Flipping the College Classroom:

Practical Advice from Faculty

Compiled and Edited by Barbi Honeycutt, PhD
Published by Magna Publications

MAGNA

Madison, Wisconsin

Magna Publications
2718 Dryden Drive
Madison, WI 53704
Magnapubs.com

Contents

Introduction

by Barbi Honeycutt, PhD

Let me begin by saying it has been privilege to be invited to write this book. Over the past five years, I have been traveling across the United States, leading workshops and speaking with faculty specifically about the flipped classroom in higher education.

Through these conversations, as well as through comments on *Faculty Focus* articles, discussions at the Teaching Professor and Teaching Professor Technology conferences, feedback from the *Faculty Focus* reader survey on Flipped Classroom Trends (2015), and through email exchanges, it's been a pleasure to learn from faculty like you who are excited about teaching. Together, we've examined the flipped classroom from a variety of perspectives. What does mean to "flip" a class? Why do it? How do you do it? When do you do it? How do you assess it? How do you get students on board? What if it doesn't work? All of these questions have helped us open a dialog about what the flip means to us, to our students, and to our disciplines. Now it's time to bring these conversations and ideas together.

When compiling this book, I reviewed all of the flipped classroom articles, videos, and course materials published by Magna Publications in recent years to bring you some of the most current thinking about the flipped classroom from the perspectives of your colleagues. Each article in the book was specifically selected to address some of the most frequently asked questions and most common challenges facing faculty who want to flip. These articles were written by educators who are exploring how the flipped classroom influences student learning and faculty success in higher education. The authors share practical advice, suggest recommendations, and offer tips to help you successfully implement the flipped approach.

Whether you've been flipping your classes for years or you're thinking about trying it for the first time, you will find recommendations and resources that are helpful for you.

Let's begin by examining the evolution of the terminology and definitions that surround any conversation about the flipped classroom.

Defining the flip

It's been an ongoing challenge to find agreement on what the flip means, where it originated, and how it is implemented. It has also been an interesting journey to watch how this educational approach has unfolded as we analyze, conceptualize, and re-analyze it in an effort to clarify our thinking and speak from common ground. Four or five years ago, many faculty asked, "What's the flipped classroom?" Fast forward a few years, and I don't hear this question as often anymore. Instead of questions, I hear reactions. Often, I hear very emotional comments such as, "The flipped classroom has changed the way I teach forever. I will never go back to the way I used to teach!" to "The flipped classroom is just a fad. It doesn't work. The students hate it!"

Like many faculty, you may be somewhere in the middle of these two extremes. Maybe you are curious about how it works. Maybe you tried it a few times. Maybe you're still trying to figure out what it means to you and your students. I think much of the debate about the flipped classroom is due to the evolving terminology as we all try to understand this approach, adapt it to our disciplines, integrate it into our courses, and keep pace with emerging scholarship. Sometimes I meet a faculty member who has not heard the term "flip" but nods knowingly when I explain the concept. The flipped approach isn't new. The term "flip" is. And the technology is. But the fundamental idea of creating an active student-centered learning environment has been around for decades.

One of the first places I was introduced to the idea of a flipped model was Lage, Platt, and Treglia's (2000) article on what they called "inverted" instruction. They explain, "Inverting the classroom means that events that have traditionally taken place inside the classroom now take place outside the classroom and vice versa. The use of learning technologies, particularly multimedia, provide new opportunities for students to learn" (Lage, Platt, and Treglia 2000, 32). Many faculty I work with are surprised to learn that the idea of the flip was introduced more than fifteen years ago in an economics journal by scholars who were on point with their thinking about how to enhance instruction with VCR tapes and a resource called the World Wide Web.

It has been a convoluted process to track down exactly who first introduced the term "flip" in relation to the flipped classroom conversation. Regardless, the term exploded throughout both K-12 and higher education settings beginning around the year 2011, specifically with help from social media and forums for teachers. Since then, the definition has started to evolve and shift.

One definition that is often cited throughout higher education is from EDUCAUSE, an organization of scholars who published their definition in 2012: "The flipped classroom is a pedagogical model in which the typical lecture and homework elements of a course are reversed. Short video lectures are viewed by students at home before the class session, while in-class time is devoted to exercises, projects, or discussions" (2012, 1)."

Around this same time, Jonathan Bergmann and Aaron Sams, two high school teachers who flip, created buzz throughout K-12 settings when their book, *Flip Your Classroom: Reach Every Student in Every Class Every Day*, was published. When asked to summarize their definition in an interview for *eSchool News*, Sams explained, "Ultimately, [it is] not about flipping the 'when and where' instruction is delivered, although that is part of it. It's about flipping the attention away from the teacher and toward the learner; it is about eliminating large-group direct instruction and meeting the individual learning needs of each student" (Bergmann and Sams 2012).

Also around this time, I developed the acronym FLIP based on my research, my teaching philosophy, and my work with faculty development. With my model, the FLIP means to "Focus on your Learners by Involving them in the Process." The FLIP is when you intentionally invert the design of a learning environment so students engage in activities, apply concepts, and focus on higher level learning processes during class (Honeycutt 2012).

In 2014, the Flipped Learning Network established a formal definition for the flip, but new language began to emerge. Instead of defining the "flipped classroom," they introduced "flipped learning" into the definition. They explain, "Flipped Learning is a pedagogical approach in which direct instruction moves from the group learning space to the individual learning space, and the resulting group space is transformed into a dynamic, interactive learning environment where the educator guides students as they apply concepts and engage creatively in the subject matter." They also conceptualized four F-L-I-P pillars of flipped learning which mean: Flexible learning environment, Learning culture, Intentional content, and Professional educator. From their perspective, these four pillars represent the foundation upon which successful flipped learning is built.

Also in 2014, Robert Talbert published a series of articles in *The Chronicle of Higher Education* where he examined the definition of the flip and shared best practices. He took the Flipped Learning Network's four F-L-I-P pillars a step further. He explained flipped learning as "a way of designing courses that emphasizes self-regulated learning and deep learning on a personal level" (Talbert 2014), adding that the definition could be expanded to include the result or product of the flip. He went on to explain that the product of this type of learning environment could be "a generation of learners who are confident, competent problem-solvers who have the abilities and the desire to learn new things on their own, throughout their lives." Talbert's definition is starting to move us beyond the "what" and "how" and into the "why."

In the *Faculty Focus* reader survey on Flipped Classroom Trends (2015), respondents were asked to define the flip in their own words. Their responses reflected the same range of interpretations we've seen from these definitions. But, after analyzing the data, we found, "[M]ost scholars and survey respondents seem to agree that active learning and student-centered learning approaches are the foundational principles of the flipped philosophy, and the value of this approach is that it can lead to enhanced student engagement, motivation, and learning, if done well" (2).

"If done well." Those three words are important as you start to think about how the flipped classroom or flipped learning model could work in your classroom.

If you jump in too quickly, you can easily get overwhelmed and burn out. You could create more anxiety and frustration among your students. You could waste time planning and designing something that didn't need to be flipped in the first place. Instead, try to take it one step at a time and make small changes. Take time to learn from others who have successfully adapted and implemented the approach in their classrooms. Hopefully, with this book, you have one more resource to help you "do it well" if you decide to flip.

Organization of this book

The book is divided into five chapters. Each chapter represents a theme from the findings in the *Faculty Focus* reader survey on Flipped Classroom Trends (2015). At the end of each chapter, you will find a set of reflection and analysis questions. These questions can be used as individual assignments to guide you through the book and plan your flipped classroom experience. These questions can also be used as part of a faculty learning community, book club, or professional development workshop to generate discussion, share ideas, and foster collaboration.

Chapter 1 focuses on the importance of organizing and planning the flipped classroom. Although the flipped classroom is a dynamic learning environment, it's important to have a plan to keep you and your students organized and on track.

Chapter 2 highlights the importance of supporting students by helping them prepare for their new role in the flipped learning environment. As they take on new responsibilities, you will need to address student motivation and possibly resistance.

Chapter 3 addresses the importance of connecting with and reaching as many of your students as you can in the flipped classroom. Consider how to include learners who may not thrive in these active learning environments as well and how to adapt your plans to serve the needs of your students in more diverse ways.

Chapter 4 focuses on assessment in the flipped classroom. When you flip, you face new challenges around grading, evaluation, and assessing learning. It's important to consider how to align assessment strategies to work with the flipped model.

Chapter 5 introduces technology into the flipped classroom conversation. Think about how technological tools can help you stay connected to and engage students before, during, and after class.

In the Conclusion, I highlight future directions to help us continue to advance the scholarship of teaching and learning specifically as it relates to flipped classrooms and flipped learning environments.

Finally, in the Tools, Templates, and Chapter Resources section, you will find bonus material you can use or adapt to help you with plan and assess your flipped classes.

Thank you for being part of this conversation. I hope this book will be a helpful resource as you think about what the flip means for you and your students.

Barbi Honeycutt, PhD
Editor and Contributing Author

CHAPTER 1

•

Organizing and Planning Learning Experiences in the Flipped Classroom

One of the most common themes that emerged from the *Faculty Focus* reader survey on Flipped Classroom Trends (2015) was the challenge of time when it comes to implementing the flipped model. Faculty are often highly motivated to try new ideas if those ideas help enhance student success and learning. But implementing new ideas takes time. It takes time to learn what the flipped classroom is, how it works, and how to adapt it to meet students' needs. It takes time to sit down and design a lesson and apply flipped strategies. It takes time to experiment with different ideas, assess them, and redesign again. It's not surprising to see "time" listed as one of the biggest barriers faculty face when planning to flip their course.

Faculty also report that they often feel overwhelmed by where to start, how to start, and how to maintain their energy and enthusiasm teaching in this type of learning environment. It can be exhausting to plan flipped learning experiences, organize group activities, and figure out how to stay organized without getting too overwhelmed or burned out.

The articles in this chapter were selected to address these challenges. These recommendations will help you focus on what to consider before you start, how to decide what to flip, and how to structure your flipped learning experiences so you save time and stay organized.

"Looking for Flippable Moments in Your Class" will help you focus on what to flip, because a surefire way to burn out is to try to flip everything!

"How to Plan a Flipped Lesson" features a four-part lesson-planning framework which helps you plan what happens before, during, and after class so you can focus on what's important and stay organized in this dynamic learning environment.

"Best Practices in Flipped Learning Design: Four Ingredients for Successful Flipped Learning" introduces four key areas to consider as you plan a flipped learning experience and integrate your activities, engagement strategies, and teaching techniques to support students.

Finally, "Avoid These Seven Rookie Mistakes When Planning to Flip Your Classroom" encourages avoiding common mistakes to help you save time and frustration. If you've been flipping your classes for a while but things aren't going as well as you expected, you may need to adjust your approach based on some of these recommendations.

Looking for Flippable Moments in Your Class

by Barbi Honeycutt, PhD

" How do you determine what can be flipped?"
With all of this discussion around flipped classrooms, more instructors are asking this question and wondering when and where flipped strategies are best integrated into the learning environment. Certainly, some topics lend themselves more easily to flipped strategies than others, but every lesson plan has the opportunity for at least one "flippable moment." This is the moment during class when you stop talking at your students and "flip" the work to them instead. This is the moment when you allow your students to struggle, ask questions, solve problems, and do the "heavy lifting" required to learn the material.

The Internet, online textbooks, online lectures, MOOCs, and other resources provide access to endless amounts of content, much of it free. Students can discover information on their own and find the answer to a question within a matter of seconds. What they can't always do on their own is analyze, synthesize, and experience the process of engaging in higher levels of critical thinking. This is when they need to do the messy work of learning, evaluating, and critiquing. This also is when they need your structure and guidance, but not your answers. They have to make meaning for themselves. This is a "flippable moment."

So, back to the original question: How do you determine what can be flipped? Here are three locations in your lesson where flipped strategies might be needed:

Flippable moment #1: Look for confusion.
Ask yourself, "What's the most difficult or challenging part of this esson?" "Where do I anticipate students having problems or encountering

difficulty?" and "Which quiz or exam questions are students consistently missing?" These are the places in your lesson that would benefit from flipped strategies. Re-think this section of your lesson and design an activity for students to engage in. Maybe they need a video to watch and re-watch several times before and after class to reinforce the main points. Maybe they need a group activity to discuss the material with their peers. Maybe they need more time to practice and test their skills. Maybe they need several opportunities to engage with the material and revisit the content using a variety of approaches.

If this is a lesson you've taught before, then you probably know where confusion is likely to occur based on student feedback from previous semesters. If you've never taught this lesson before, consider adding a classroom assessment technique to the middle or end of your lesson so you can design a flipped learning experience when students need it the most. This will allow both you and your students to determine where additional work is needed to achieve the learning outcomes.

Flippable moment #2: Look for the fundamentals.

Ask yourself, "What's the most fundamental, most essential, and most critical part of today's lesson?" "What MUST students know before they can move forward?" Some may argue fundamental knowledge isn't what needs to be flipped, but if this is an essential skill your students need to develop before moving on, then it might be the perfect place to flip your approach. Your challenge is to design multiple learning opportunities and create a
variety of opportunities where students can practice, test, and reinforce their knowledge to ensure mastery.

Flippable moment #3: Look for boredom.

Ask yourself, "Are the students bored?" "Am I bored?" Boredom will destroy a learning environment. If your students are bored, they are not likely to participate. When you are bored, you're not bringing your best energy and ideas to the classroom and your students will notice. That's when it's time to mix things up. When you come to a point in your lesson or course when boredom strikes, it's time to flip your approach. Design a task for your students to *do*. Instead of continuing to lecture to them, take an "actively passive" approach and step to the side. Put students in pairs or groups. Pose a challenge. Allow them to design or evaluate something. Give them the space to struggle, practice, and imagine "what if?" so they are challenged and inspired. That's the power of the flip.

Many instructors sit down to plan a lesson and begin with the question, "What am I going to talk about today?" Flip that thinking. When you sit down to plan your flipped lesson, always begin by asking yourself, "What do students need to *do* to achieve the learning outcomes for this lesson?" Then find flippable moments to help you focus.

To learn what you know now as an instructor, you had to do the "heavy lifting" yourself. You had to analyze, reflect, and evaluate. You had to make meaning for yourself. Now it's your students' turn. Flip it to them.

Reprinted from *Faculty Focus,* March 25, 2013.

How to Plan a Flipped Lesson

by Barbi Honeycutt, PhD

Since the flipped classroom is a dynamic and interactive space, it's important to bring structure and organization to your planning process. Although it may seem like "dynamic" and "organized" are complete opposites, you need both to create a successful flipped learning experience for your students.

The importance of planning

If flipped activities are assigned without structure and organization, you'll create a chaotic environment and students will quickly become frustrated. This is probably one of the main comments I hear from students who had negative experiences in flipped classrooms. If they don't know what to do or what is expected of them, then they will not see the benefits of this type of learning environment. By having a plan, you—and your students— know what is expected, what the goal is, and how to determine if the goal was met. Planning can include creating a lesson plan complete with learning outcomes, activities, and assessment strategies. Planning also includes the processes and systems you put into place to help you manage paperwork, group discussions, and the overall classroom environment.

The importance of flexibility

At the same time, if you are overly organized or too rigid with your plan, you will likely lose sight of the powerful learning moments that often emerge in flipped learning environments. Give yourself—and your students—the opportunity to explore a path of conversation or pursue a line of thinking that might not fit directly into your perfectly well developed plan. Knowing when to take a conversation in a different direction from your intended learning outcomes without getting too far off topic takes experience and some finesse, but the point is to allow for these moments by being flexible and allowing time for this type of exploration when you can.

The four-part flipped lesson plan

If you're new to flipped and active learning approaches, or if you've been struggling with how to successfully implement this model in your classes, the best advice is to start with just one lesson. When you start planning to flip one lesson, you can experiment with different ideas and strategies to get a feel for your changing role in this type of learning environment. It does take a new set of skills to be the "guide on the side" as you help students work through the course material at their own pace. By starting with one lesson, you can avoid getting too overwhelmed by trying to do too much too fast.

To begin, one way to organize the flipped learning experience is to create a lesson plan (Honeycutt and Garrett 2013). There are many formats for creating lesson plans, but I like to use the Flipped Lesson Plan template—located at the end of the book—which I created to help map the learning outcomes and activities before, during, and after class time. In this template, there are four parts to the flipped lesson planning process: (1) the purpose, (2) the prior-to-class activities, (3) the in-class activities, and (4) the closing.

Before you begin, ask yourself, "What do students need to *do* to achieve the learning outcomes?" Note that you are not planning what *you* will say or do right now. Keep the focus on the students. Then, as you start thinking about which lesson you'd like to flip, consider each of these four areas:

Purpose

What is the purpose of your lesson? It may seem like an obvious answer to you, but most students will need to know the goal. Ask yourself, "What should students be able to do at the end of the lesson?" Focus on the lesson you are flipping, not the whole course. Write the purpose statement as a learning outcome using language that is specific and measurable. Fill in the blank: By the end of this lesson, students will be able to _____. The more specific and measurable the purpose statement, the more successful you will be in clarifying your expectations, creating learning activities, and developing assessments.

Prior-to-class

What will students do prior to coming to class? What should they have accomplished or completed before they begin the in-class activities you have planned? And how will you know if they actually did it? You need to have a strategy for holding students accountable for completing the prior-to-class work. Consider using classroom assessment techniques such as quizzing, minute papers, or forum posts to make the completion of the prior-to-class work visible. Keep the prior-to-class activities focused on the lower level learning outcomes so you can dedicate the in-class time to addressing the higher level learning outcomes (Honeycutt and Garrett 2013). If you are using the Flipped Lesson Plan template and you've mapped each level of Bloom's Taxonomy, you will be able to see which learning outcomes need to be completed prior to coming to class. Then you can create an assignment to help students achieve those outcomes so they are prepared to participate when they arrive to class.

In-class

When students arrive to class, what will they be expected to do? With the flipped model, the in-class time should be designed so students are engaging in activities connected specifically to the higher level learning outcomes. What are students analyzing, evaluating, or creating? What problems are they solving? Are they using their laptops, tablets, workbooks, or textbooks? Are they in groups? What is the purpose of the group activity? How does the group's input improve students' ability to actually achieve the learning outcomes? Always select flipped strategies based on what types of activities and tasks help the students achieve the learning outcomes. Otherwise, students may see the activity as "busy work" and they may not take it seriously. As you and your students become more comfortable and confident with the flipped model, you can design more interactive learning experiences for other lessons.

Closing

How will the lesson end? In the flipped learning environment, students are often moving at different paces as they work through the course material, solve problems, and share ideas within their groups. For this reason, it's important to make sure everyone is on the same page as you prepare to end class. Revisit your learning outcomes and help students determine which ones they achieved and what content is still causing confusion. You could end class with a quiz, a summary, or a preview of the homework assignment as they prepare for the next lesson. You could end the class by revisiting the learning outcomes and reminding students what they achieved and why it matters. The key is to bring the lesson to a meaningful close and ensure all students are prepared as they leave one lesson and move on to the next.

By addressing these four areas, you can begin to organize the flipped lesson plan and connect the prior-to-class work to the in-class activities. The planning process helps keep you and your students focused and on task.

Best Practices in Flipped Learning Design: Four Ingredients for Successful Flipped Learning

by Robert Talbert, PhD

Effective flipped learning environments require careful attention to the design of those environments. Four ingredients that go into a successful design are **structure** (in this case, backward design), **rich resources** (such as video, audio, or games), **engagement** (which requires determining the zone of proximal development), and **communication** (including assessment, informal evaluations, and human-to-human discourse). Read on for more on each of these ingredients.

1. Structure

Use a "backward design" model (popularized by Grant Wiggins and Jay McTighe in their book *Understanding by Design*) for course design in which you first identify the results desired from students, *then* determine what would constitute acceptable evidence of mastery of those results, and *then* plan learning experiences and instruction to give students the opportunity to produce this evidence (Wiggins and McTighe 2005).

The diagram on the next page shows how Wiggins and McTighe's original backward design model can be adapted to flipped learning design of a single lesson:

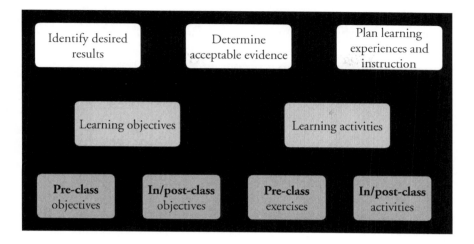

When determining the desired learning outcomes and the evidence that would be sufficient to show mastery of those outcomes, create a list of **learning objectives** that codify exactly what you want to see students do. Those learning objectives (phrased as action verbs whose outcomes can be measured—avoiding verbs like "know" or "understand") can be further split into **basic** objectives (what students can and should address prior to class meetings in their individual spaces) and **advanced** objectives (what students can and should address in the group space, when having the instructor and classmates at hand is the most helpful).

Then, when planning the learning experiences and instruction and looking back at what constitutes acceptable evidence of learning, design **learning activities**, some of which take place **pre-class** as students encounter new concepts for the first time, and others which take place **in class** and **after class** where higher-level cognitive tasks are addressed.

2. Rich resources

Having determined the learning objectives and activities for a lesson, provide students with a rich set of high-quality resources that they can use to learn, as an archive for later review, and as an opportunity to engage in self-regulated learning. These can include:

- A textbook or other source of reading
- Video
- Audio
- Games
- Computer simulations

Note that **flipped learning does not require the use of video**, nor should you limit the kind of media students use to just one or two types. Take a **"both/and" approach**, giving students a wide range of options and letting them choose freely from among the resources provided (and even the option to include their own resources).

3. Engagement

Lev Vygotksy's (Gredler 2008) concept of the **zone of proximal development** (ZPD) tells us that we can expect the best results from learning activities when they land in the zone between those tasks that students can do unaided and those tasks that the students cannot do. These are the tasks that the student *can do with guidance*. Each student has his or her own ZPD for a given subject, and the scope of this ZPD changes as students learn. To maximize the probability of fruitful engagement with a task, we have to have a sense of where the "center of gravity" of a class' collected ZPD lies and target the learning activities there. Knowing where each student's ZPD is at a given time requires the final ingredient:

4. Communication

There are three kinds of communication that are valuable in any class but especially in a flipped learning environment:

- *Assessment results.* Frequent, lightweight formative assessment can provide data on what students know and the items with which they are struggling, even if students have no questions or choose not to voice questions. Giving such assessments to "take the temperature" of the class every day, even in between class days, is crucial for knowing whether the learning activities are pitched correctly and the extent to which learning objectives are being met.
- *Informal course evaluations.* We usually give course evaluations once a term, but it's important to get student input on the conduct of the course and on their learning process regularly. Students sometimes are rather uncomfortable or uncertain in a flipped learning environment, and this can interfere with learning; giving students multiple opportunities to voice their questions and concerns helps you in the long run and helps students in the short term. Giving informal course evaluations two to four times during a semester through a simple paper or online survey is all you need to gather this information.
- *Human-to-human discourse.* Of course there's no substitute for actual human-to-human communication. Flipped learning environments

allow an unprecedented chance for instructors to communicate with each student, or at least each group of students, in every class meeting and build a "client-consultant" relationship where students and their learning processes are valued.

An example of a guided practice assignment is included at the end of this book.

Adapted from the Magna Online Seminar presentation, *Best Practices in Flipped Class Design*.

Avoid These Seven Rookie Mistakes When Planning to Flip Your Classroom

by Barbi Honeycutt, PhD

There's so much buzz about the flipped classroom model. From K-12 to higher education settings, from corporate training to continuing education, instructors around the world are talking about how to use inverted instructional design to engage students and improve the learning experience. It's easy to get caught up in the excitement!

However, as I travel across the U.S. and speak with educators, it's not uncommon for me to hear:

"I tried it and it didn't work at all," or "Students hated it," or "It took too much time," or "I'm never doing THAT again!"

When I hear responses like these, I always dig a little deeper. Almost every single time, I can pinpoint that at least one of these "rookie" mistakes resulted in a poor flipped learning experience for both the faculty and the students:

Rookie mistake #1: Narrowly defining what the flipped classroom is.

"What's your definition of the flipped classroom?" This is the first question I always ask faculty when they say the flipped classroom doesn't work. If you only define the flipped classroom as "students watching videos of lectures before class" then yes, your flipped classroom will fail. Expand your definition.

In my work, the FLIP means to "Focus on your Learners by Involving them in the Process." Involve students in higher level learning and critical thinking experiences *during* class time. Move the lower level learning experiences *outside* of class time. When you define it this way, videos may be one tool to use to help students master content prior to coming to class, but there are many other tools and strategies that will work more effectively.

Rookie mistake #2: Poorly articulated learning outcomes.

You must clarify your learning outcomes for both the pre-class and in-class learning activities. If your students cannot show you the result of the learning activity, then you need to rewrite your learning outcomes. Get focused. Be specific. Learning outcomes must be measurable.

If you cannot articulate what students need to be able to do, then they will be confused and frustrated. If that happens, they will not do the pre-class work or engage in the activities you have planned during class. Review Bloom's Taxonomy to help you clarify learning outcomes. Share the learning outcomes with your students. Use worksheets, templates, and other tools to organize the flipped learning experience, focus attention, and clarify why the activity, assignment, or task matters.

Rookie mistake #3: Not planning.

One of the most important responsibilities you have as a teacher in the flipped classroom is to plan. Plan the learning outcomes. Create a lesson plan. Plan each step of the activities you will use in class. Plan how you will introduce the flipped activity at the beginning of class. Plan how you will navigate to each group to answer students' questions. Plan how many markers, whiteboards, flip charts, or worksheets you need. Plan how much time you think it will take to complete the activity.

The flipped classroom is a dynamic place. It's noisy. Students are talking, sharing ideas, and solving problems. Some students are using their phone to find answers. Some are using the book. Students in one group are working at a different pace than students in another group. Planning is critical to organizing this type of learning environment. On the flip side (pun intended!) of this mistake, it is possible to plan too much, so be careful. You still need to be flexible and adaptable within your plan, but as the saying goes, "Failing to plan is planning to fail."

Rookie mistake #4: The activity is too big.

When you think about the flipped activities students will participate in during class, it's easy to get excited and go for the "big" ones. Maybe you design a complex case study, an awesome game, or a detailed simulation. These types of activities address the highest levels of critical thinking, so they require more time during class, more planning before class, and more of you.

If you're new to the FLIP, and you're just starting to try active learning strategies in your classes, then go for an activity with a lower level of intensity. Use flipped activities that are less complex until you build your confidence and understand the nuances of student-centered learning. Once you gain more experience with the model, then go for the more intense flipped activities.

Rookie mistake #5: Flipping everything.

Don't flip everything! If a lesson is working well and students are meeting or exceeding expectations, leave it alone. You don't need to spend your energy or time redesigning it to fit within the flipped model. Instead, look for the places where students are confused or struggling with the course material. Look for those flippable moments. Where are your students are bored? Where are they confused? Where are *you* bored? Those are the places in your course and in a lesson where the flip is needed.

Rookie mistake #6: Forgetting to prepare students for their changing role.

Just as you are learning to teach this way, your students are learning how to learn this way. Clearly communicate your expectations and be willing to adjust as needed to support students as they gain more confidence with their new role in the flipped learning environment. They may need more structure upfront. They may have more questions. They may be resistant or hesitant to just jump right in and participate.

Explain their new roles and responsibilities. Challenge them with new tasks and push them out of their comfort zones, but be supportive when you do it. Provide the resources and tools to help them succeed. The flipped model is not about leaving students alone while they struggle and figure it all out for themselves. In fact, it's quite the opposite. Which leads me to the next rookie mistake...

Rookie mistake #7: Forgetting to prepare for your changing role.

Some instructors are unprepared or uncertain about what to do in class if they're not lecturing. When you plan your lesson, ask yourself "what are students going to do?" and then map it out. Then step back and reflect on how your role will change.

You will not spend the majority of your time lecturing from the front of the room. You will be teaching from the sidelines, becoming that "guide on the side" as students work through the assignment and activities. You will have to get more comfortable with releasing control in the classroom as students work in groups, move at different paces, and ask questions you may not expect. Think about your role carefully and decide how comfortable you are with these challenges. For some instructors, this is an easy and welcome transition. For others, it's extremely stressful and difficult. Be honest about who you are as a teacher and how this model fits into your teaching philosophy and style.

Final thoughts

As you start thinking about implementing flipped strategies into your classroom, think about how you can avoid these seven rookie mistakes. If you've been teaching using the flipped model for a while but you're still not finding the success you want, review these mistakes again and see if they apply to your course.

And remember, change takes time. Be flexible and patient with yourself and with your students. Not all flipped lessons will be successful. There will be resistance from students. There will be activities that miss the mark. There will be lessons when the activity you designed just didn't fit the learning outcomes. But there will also be flipped lessons that end with awesome results that allow you to why you do what you do.

CHAPTER 1 REFLECTION AND DISCUSSION QUESTIONS

Use these questions for reflection, discussion, and application as you consider how to organize and plan successful flipped classroom learning experiences.

Reflection and Discussion:
1. What do you need to plan and prepare for as you think about implementing the flipped model in your courses?
2. We're all concerned about the limited amount of time we have to plan, design, and redesign our courses. What timesaving strategies could you implement to make the process of flipping a course or lesson less time-consuming? What processes can be automated? What tools can you use to help you with planning?
3. How can you help students manage their in-class and out-of-class time so they aren't overwhelmed with the flipped learning experience? What tools or resources can you share with them to help them plan, do the pre-class work, and be successful as a learner in the flipped classroom?

Application:
1. Think about one of your courses you'd like to flip. Then, focus on one lesson within that course. Maybe it's a lesson that hasn't been working well and you'd like to redesign it. Try to locate the flippable moments within that lesson. Describe them to help you start focusing on what and when to flip.
2. Once you locate the flippable moments, write two or three learning objectives at the basic and advanced levels.
3. Then brainstorm what types of learning activities students will participate in and consider where those learning activities will occur (before, during, or after class).
4. Identify the types of media and resources students will use for this part of the lesson.
5. Brainstorm the types of assessment activities you could integrate into this lesson.

CHAPTER 2

•

Supporting Students: Preparation, Motivation, and Resistance in the Flipped Classroom

The most frequently asked question about the flipped classroom is, "How do I get students to do the pre-class work and come to class prepared?" No doubt about it, this is a challenge all educators face regardless of the type of instructional model used. But the flipped classroom magnifies this problem because it relies on the students coming to class ready to engage in active learning situations where they apply the information from the pre-class work.

Related to this question, instructors ask how to address student resistance when students either choose not to engage or become outright confrontational. Students may resist this type of learning environment because it's new and they are uncertain about it, or because they have had a negative experience with this type of instructional approach. Interestingly, more problems arise when students think they know what the flipped classroom is only to find out you are conceptualizing it a different way. This is why it's so important to know what the flipped classroom means to you, how you define it, and how to implement it in your classroom.

And finally, students may also bring negative associations with group work and collaborative projects into your classroom. These prior experiences can make the flipped classroom model even more challenging to implement. Group work is usually an essential part of the flipped learning experience whether you use groups for in-class activities or for long term projects throughout a semester.

This chapter focuses on how to support students through these processes so they can see the value of this type of learning experience. The authors share strategies to manage student resistance, address student motivation and preparation, and overcome the challenges of group work in the flipped classroom.

"Three Critical Conversations Started and Sustained by Flipped Learning" is designed to help you start conversations with your students about the flipped model and address some of the potential areas that cause student resistance.

"Five Ways to Motivate Unprepared Students in the Flipped Classroom" addresses the challenge of motivating students to come to class prepared and ready to participate.

"I Don't Like this One Little Bit: Engaging Students in a Flipped Classroom" offers a closer look at how to create flipped classroom environments that engage students and address some of the challenges of getting students on board with this approach.

"Ready to Flip: Three Ways to Hold Students Accountable for Pre-Class Work" addresses the most commonly asked question about the flipped classroom: "How do we get students to come to class prepared?"

In the fifth and sixth articles, the author shares recommendations and strategies to help you create and manage successful small group learning experiences in the flipped classroom.

Three Critical Conversations Started and Sustained by Flipped Learning

by Robert Talbert, PhD

The flipped learning model of instruction has begun to make the transition from an educational buzzword to a normative practice among many university instructors, and with good reason. Flipped learning provides many benefits for both faculty and students. However, instructors who use flipped learning soon find out that a significant amount of work is sometimes necessary to win students over to this way of conducting class. Even when the benefits of flipped learning are made clear to students, some of them will still resist. And to be fair, many instructors fail to listen to what students are really saying.

Many student complaints about flipped learning reveal important questions about teaching and learning that deserve to be brought to the surface because of the flipped environment. Here are three common issues raised by students and the conversation-starters they afford.

Student comment: "I wish you would just teach the class."

Conversation-starter: Why do we have classes?

This issue is often raised once it becomes clear that class time will focus on assimilating information, not transmitting it. For many students, the only kind of instruction they have ever known is the in-class lecture, so it is quite natural for them to conflate "teaching" and "lecturing." Hence, students are perhaps justifiably unsettled to see their teacher not "teaching."

When students raise this concern, it is an opportunity to have a conversation about why classes meet—or for that matter, why they exist—in the first place. When students want the professor to "just teach," the professor can pose the following: "We can either have lecture on basic information in class, and then you will be responsible for the harder parts yourselves outside of class, or we can make the basic information available for you prior to class, and spend our class time making sense of the harder parts. There is not enough class time for both. Which setup will help you learn better?"

Student comment: "I learn best through listening to a lecture."

Conversation-starter: How does one learn?

Students who have made it through secondary schooling believe that since lecturing "worked" in the sense that they made it to college under a lecture-centric system, lecture is the most effective means of teaching—in fact, the only means of teaching that "works." (Indeed, many university instructors believe the same thing.)

I respond to this with a question: "What are the three most important things you have ever learned?" Here are my three: speaking my native language, feeding myself, and going to the bathroom. When the student comes up with his or her list, I follow up: "How did you learn those things?" The answer is always that it's a mixture of a bit of direct instruction (which is largely ignored), along with a lot of trial and error and peer pressure. No student has ever responded that they learned these things only by listening to a lecture. No student ever will!

If a person has demonstrated repeatedly that he or she can learn important things in life without lecture, on what basis does he or she say that they learn best through lecture? Maybe the ability to learn on one's own is more deeply connected to one's humanity than we suspect. Which brings up the last issue:

Student comment: "I shouldn't have to teach myself the subject."

Conversation-starter: Why are we here?

In the flipped classroom, students are expected to gain fluency with basic ideas in preparation for class time, rather than as the result of class time. It is easy for a student to see this as self-teaching and respond negatively. A variant of this is, "I'm paying you to teach me!" At its core, this is not an issue about who is paying whom, but about the purpose of higher education.

We might approach the student simply by asking: "What is the purpose of college? Why are you here?" Among the more noble answers include career preparation, personal growth, and obtaining life experiences. What do these good things have in common? I am convinced that each student's reasons for being in college will intersect at the notion of learning how to learn. Career success, meaningful growth, and formative experiences all involve acquiring the ability and the taste for learning new things, independently and throughout one's lifespan. Why not start that process now?

It's easy to be defensive when, as an instructor, students voice seemingly belligerent opposition to the flipped classroom. But if we listen closely, we'll hear those complaints as invitations to important conversations that can shape student learning for the better.

Reprinted from *Faculty Focus,* March 2, 2015.

Five Ways to Motivate Unprepared Students in the Flipped Classroom

by Barbi Honeycutt, PhD

"What if students don't do the work?" I've been traveling the country for the past five years leading faculty development workshops. When it comes to the flipped classroom, I am asked this question in every single workshop at every single campus I visit. And rightly so! After all, the flipped classroom model—or any active, student-centered learning model—relies heavily on students being prepared and ready to engage in the learning activities. If students are unprepared, then it limits what they can do, how deeply they can engage with the material, and how meaningfully they can connect with other students. It also challenges you to determine how to proceed. Do you give a quick lecture to recap the pre-class content so everyone is on the same page? Do you give the unprepared students an alternative assignment? Do you kick them out of class? Do they earn an "F" in the course?

Your response to this question is based on your teaching philosophy and the type of classroom environment you want to create. For many readers, I would guess the answer to all of these questions is probably "no." Many of us would prefer to proactively design the learning environment using strategies to promote learning and personal development instead of relying on punitive measures to change behavior.

So, what can we do to address the challenge of unprepared students? Here are five recommendations to start the discussion:

1. Have a conversation.

Before you react too quickly, take a few days to identify exactly who is not prepared. Is it the same two or three students each time? Is it the same group or team of students? Do you see a trend? Are they only unprepared on Mondays, for example? Are the students resistant? Are they genuinely worried about not completing the assignment? Keep a record, and then have a conversation with the students. Ask them to make arrangements to stay after the next class. (Don't ask them to stay after today's class because they are most likely not prepared to do so and that will just create more friction between you and the students.)

Sometimes all it takes is a conversation with a student to find out what's going on and why they are falling behind. Then make a plan together to move forward. Once they realize they're on your radar, you may not need to do anything else.

2. Review your pre-class assignment.

The flipped classroom is a partnership. You and your students are working together. Your role is to design the learning experience. Their role is to come to class ready to participate in the learning experience. You plan the activities. They engage in the activities. You teach by guiding from the side. They learn by doing. One of your responsibilities is to design the pre-class assignment. Is it clear what the students are supposed to do? Is it too demanding? Does it take too much time? Is it confusing? Could it be organized more effectively? Sometimes a simple adjustment in the pre-class assignment is all you need to improve student preparedness.

3. Proceed as planned.

If you give a quick lecture to recap the pre-class work, you will be giving a quick lecture in every class from now on. Try not to fall back to that approach. Proceed with your activities just as you planned. This will show unprepared students that class time will not be derailed by their lack of preparation. Be sure to show students the value of the pre-class work. How are they using the pre-class work during class time? How does the pre-class work help them finish the in-class work more efficiently and effectively? What parts of the pre-class work are being applied during class time? How are you recognizing students for their preparation? The unprepared students will see the value of the pre-class work and hopefully this will motivate them to be prepared next time. And, if your activities rely on group work, use the power of peer pressure. Most group members will not tolerate someone being chronically unprepared.

4. Rethink participation grades.

If you build in participation grades as part of your grading policy, then make "completing pre-class work" a significant part of the participation and final grade. This will give you more flexibility in determining what counts as "participation" and how you choose to respond. This approach also permits students to have more control over their choice in whether to come prepared. They know the consequences in terms of how their lack of preparation affects their grade. You may consider other policies such as a free pass on one pre-class assignment. After all, life happens. Even your best, brightest, and most well-prepared students can have an off day.

5. Set up a corner.

A couple of years ago, I led a faculty development workshop at a university, and one of the faculty members shared this strategy for managing unprepared students: She said she had success setting up a corner in the front of the room where students who did not complete the pre-class work would go to finish their assignment during class time. This approach allowed students to catch up, but if the pre-class assignment took longer to complete than class time, then they had to figure out a way to complete the in-class work on their own time.

When students are unprepared for the learning activities, it can cause stress for both you and the other students in the room. With these five recommendations, hopefully you can address why students aren't prepared and help support them in recognizing their role and their responsibilities in this type of learning environment.

Reprinted from *Faculty Focus*, April 4. 2016.

I Don't Like This One Little Bit: Engaging Students in a Flipped Classroom

by Penne Restad, PhD

The Internet flipped learning before instructors did. Want to find out something? Google it. Wikipedia it. Use your laptop or smartphone or iPad. That's where the "answers" are. Some of us initially reacted to this cyber-democratization of information asserting, "This isn't right! The Internet is full of incomplete and simply wrong information." But the challenge to the classroom is more profound.

We can feel nostalgic for some lost past when students did their work because we assigned it, when we could espouse the importance of "learning for learning's sake," when our place at the lectern elicited deference, when we could tend the gates of knowledge fairly effectively. While those days, if they ever existed, are gone, the authentic values of the classroom encounter remain.

In fact, I would argue that they have become even more important. Students more than ever need to develop and practice the skills needed to navigate vast amounts of data, to select, evaluate, connect, and draw conclusions about the barrage of information available to us all. This (fairly) new state of affairs requires us to move from our often implicit understandings of what constitutes teaching to find explicit ways to put the information revolution at the service of what we know to be our core tasks.

The challenge can be energizing. We strive to inculcate in our students the methods and values associated with our particular disciplines as well as the knowledge and understanding about how and what we seek to glean from information. We work to create for them the passions that brought us to our work. We are no longer the sole sources of information and interpretation, but that only underlines the importance of engaging students in the process of critical thinking and interpretation. If we are successful, they will be better prepared for their own successes.

Flipping for team-based learning

There are many wonderfully creative and effective ways to design classes that address the new landscapes of learning. Many take advantage of a combination of online and in-class learning—using strategies that have variously been called flipped, blended, hybrid, disruptive, or, by the time this book is published, by some new term. Most aim to incorporate online and out-of-classroom tools (like the old-fashioned reading assignment) to foster a more effective learning environment.

My version of a "flipped" class, an American history survey course of 80 students, is based on a Team-Based Learning (TBL) platform. Students prepare for class by reading online materials—portions of texts, sets of primary documents, interpretive pieces, study guides—and writing short online journal responses. The pre-work arms them with at least a passing familiarity with key narratives, interpretations and concepts, and positions them for doing more difficult and interactive work in class.

In class, students gather in permanently assigned teams of six or seven where they discuss, probe, and more fully develop their recently acquired knowledge. I have developed templates with sequenced questions or tasks that direct them into a deeper understanding of course concepts and content. Each template is different, but focuses on a selection of skills related to studying history. One template, for example, asks a team to rank primary sources they've just read. Which is most important for understanding the political climate of that era? Which is least biased in its presentation of facts? How does your experience of the present affect how you understand these documents? Another prompts students to identify the shared assumptions and values represented in a small collection of time-related documents. As the teams work in class, I eavesdrop and sometimes participate in a local discussion. On occasion, I will interrupt the class to clarify a point, and sometimes a "teachable moment" inspires a short, impromptu lecture. The teams' conclusions reached at various stages of a template provide the basis for class-wide discussions; when we compare notes, we challenge each other to defend our answers. These are opportunities for me to draw out the most important ideas the teams have uncovered and to offer my own expertise in order to provide a more complete understanding of the collective analyses.

Splitting the learning venue between online preparation and the classroom interaction and shifting the responsibility for learning the basic course information onto the student, alters the instructor's role from being on the stage to setting it.

For some instructors, this is no small adjustment, but I've found two keys to making it work. One, stake your expertise on assembling the materials and sequence, to lay down the breadcrumbs that will allow students to pick up the trail. This is a process of the well-known concept of backward design. What skills and knowledge do you want the students to learn to do? What steps will you design to allow them to practice? Two, participate along with the class. Enjoy the noisy discussion of the teams. Be ready to give a five-minute flash lecture to address any confusion you discover while circulating through the room. Challenge one team to defend its conclusions against those of another. Build on the class's insights by making a well-timed observation or summation that furthers the conversation. Give students credit. Teams most likely won't arrive at perfect answers, but the class of teams will reveal an array of answers and responses that might surprise, please, and engage you.

Not surprisingly, students can be wary when they walk into such a class. They know that their polite and passive attention is expected in the lecture hall. College students also have been known to voice the opinion that they did group work in the fourth grade, and now want the "college experience." Yet, in a flipped class, they will find it difficult to be successful if they sit quietly as passive observers of the learning process. They have to be actively involved. They have to take risks, engage in conversation, defend their ideas, and listen to others. A class built on thinking about information is more work than listening to information, and it can be noisy. Since teams are constructed to reflect diverse thinking (a senior chemistry major and a sophomore fine arts major, for example, might end up on the same team), there are often disagreements. Disagreement is encouraged—and investigated. Memorization won't solve anything—let alone ensure a good grade.

One student neatly summed up a not-uncommon reaction to the setting in which the focus is on the subject and not on the teacher. He announced at the beginning of the semester, "I don't like this one little bit." He didn't like the idea that he had to talk to people who weren't in his discipline. He didn't like the idea that he had to reach a consensus with his team. He didn't like that I wasn't lecturing him on what he had to know in order to get a good grade. That was the first week. By the second week, he'd decided to give it a try. At the end of the term, he told me he (a science major) saw the value in discussing and arguing about the primary sources and historical meaning. For many, the experience of testing out ideas and working on a higher level of thinking is engaging, lively, and thought-provoking.

Students, just like the rest of us, want to succeed and often grow concerned when put in a new situation. I've relied on a few strategies to help students adjust to a flipped class and also to see its value.

Students will encounter team-based work in their chosen careers, a point I emphasize early. In class, students are practicing getting their own best ideas and evidence forward and collaborating with others to find answers. They will also need to work out interpersonal tensions, establish workflows, make constructive suggestions, and be accountable to the team effort.

Expect that not all of a team's talk will be exactly on point. Keep in mind that students are working on the social aspects of knowledge building. I've noticed that teams can build healthy bonds that carry beyond the classroom.

Your attitude matters. Be confident and remain positive. There will be moments in which a lesson will not go smoothly. Because you cannot anticipate and prepare a fully formed lecture on each point, you will find you may just have to admit you cannot answer a particular question. On the other hand, teams often come up with a new perspective, which gives you an opportunity to model how you are evaluating their point in light of your own expertise. This is a good opportunity to share with the class the importance of flexibility and thinking on your feet.

Finally, to repeat a point mentioned above, enjoy the class. Your engagement in the topic and in the students' exploration is contagious and critical to students trusting that their active learning won't hurt them—or their GPA.

This is a just a brief explanation of one way to flip a class—and to get students to be willing participants. There are many others. Yet the main elements are the same: 1) The instructor uses technology in some way—YouTube, PowerPoint, lectures, linked sources, etc.—to acquaint students with course concepts and content before they arrive in class. 2) He or she then uses class time to help students gain a deeper understanding of the material.

In the end, the benefits of the flipped approach are considerable. Students take more responsibility for their own learning. Working in class along with a master of the discipline (you), they learn to think more critically, communicate more effectively, and have a greater appreciation for the unique importance and logic of the subject. And they experience at least some of the satisfaction of learning how to think in a new, and, in some cases, life-changing way.

Reprinted from *Faculty Focus,* July 22, 2013.

Ready to Flip: Three Ways to Hold Students Accountable for Pre-Class Work

by Barbi Honeycutt, PhD

One of the most frequently asked questions about the flipped classroom model is: "How do you encourage students to actually do the pre-class work and come to class prepared?"

This is not really a new question for educators. We've always assigned some type of homework, and there have always been students who do not come to class ready to learn. However, the flipped classroom conversation has launched this question straight to the top of the list of challenges faculty face when implementing this model in their classrooms. By design, the flipped model places more emphasis on the importance of homework or pre-class work to ensure that in-person class time is effective, allowing the instructor and the students to explore higher levels of application and analysis together. If students are unprepared, it leads to frustration, stress, and anxiety for everyone (Honeycutt 2016b).

First, let's clarify what we mean by a "flipped" classroom. Findings from the *Faculty Focus* reader survey on Flipped Classroom Trends (2015), clearly show there are many variations and interpretations of what "flipped" means in higher education. For many educators, the definition of a flipped classroom moves beyond one that uses videos as the only instructional tool. In my work, FLIP means to "Focus on your Learners by Involving them in the Process." In this model, the pre-class work focuses on the lower levels of Bloom's Taxonomy and the in-class work focuses on the higher levels of Bloom's Taxonomy. I encourage faculty to integrate active learning strategies to involve learners in the process of applying, analyzing, and creating knowledge during class time. Students work through foundational material prior to class so the time spent in class with their peers and the instructor becomes more valuable as they explore higher levels of critical thinking and analysis.

Make your expectations clear

The flipped classroom—or any active learning environment—often demands students come to class "prepared." What do you mean when you say you want students to be prepared? How do you know if they are prepared? In the flipped classroom, it's critical for the instructor to clarify exactly what being prepared means and what the expectations are.

For example, if you assign a chapter for your students to "read before class" or tell them to "come to class prepared to discuss the chapter," what exactly are you expecting students to be able to do? Can you be more specific? What information will be used during class time? How will it be used? What details are important? Do students need to know how to define all the terminology in the chapter so they can use it to analyze a case study during class? Do you want them to be able to answer review questions at the end of the chapter to prepare for a class discussion? Do you want them to be able to compare two points of view from the chapter as part of an in-class debate?

Many instructors use video in their flipped classrooms. The same questions apply. It's not enough to say "watch the video" and expect students to magically know what to look for, identify what's important, and understand why it matters. What do you want students to do while watching, or after watching, the video? Do they need to answer questions before, during, and after the video? As they watch the video, should they pause it at key points and complete a task before proceeding? Do they need to fill in a worksheet, draw a process, or solve a problem shown in the video? Is it clear how the information in the video will help them succeed when they are in class?

Hold students accountable

Once you clarify what you want students to actually *do* prior to class, then what? How will you hold them accountable? How will they hold themselves and each other accountable? To address this challenge, here are a few strategies you can integrate into your flipped class to help clarify what you want students to be able to do, to connect the pre-class assignment to the beginning of in-class time, and to make visible who is prepared in order to help you hold them accountable for completing the pre-class work:

1. Ticket to enter

If you asked students to complete a task as part of their pre-class work, make sure it's something they can bring with them and use as a "ticket" to enter class that day. For example, ask students to write three questions they have from the video or reading, including the time stamps or page numbers that correspond to their questions. As they enter the classroom, ask them to hand in their ticket to enter class. Bonus: After you collect all the tickets, you can use them as part of a small group activity, to review for a test, or to start a class discussion.

2. Choose a side

This strategy works best if your pre-class work involves two points of view, an argument, or opposing interpretations of a topic related to the course material. In the pre-class work, send them a question or comment they need to be prepared to take a stance on. For example, suppose your pre-class reading or video showcases two researchers presenting different sides of a case involving stem cell research. On one wall of your classroom, post a sign with the name of one of the researchers. Then post the name of the other researcher on the other wall. As students enter class, ask them to write their name on a sticky note and post their note on the wall with the name of the researcher they believe had the best argument. Bonus: This is can be a strategy for taking attendance too.

3. Pass-the-problem resource sheet

If you have several problems, cases, or scenarios you want students to solve or analyze, try the pass-the-problem flipped strategy in class. To prepare for this activity, ask students to come to class with a one-page resource sheet (sometimes called a "cheat sheet") which will be the only resource they can use to solve the problem. I've seen this strategy used during final exams, often in courses requiring high levels of memorization. Using the cheat sheet in this way, however, allows students to collaborate and develop sheets as a group rather than as individuals. They will be held accountable both as a team member and as an individual. This activity could be combined with the "ticket to enter" strategy as well.

These teaching strategies combine assessment, accountability, and active learning into one learning experience for students. Preparing for these questions and activities challenges you to take your directions about pre-class work one step further to specify exactly what you want the students to *do* with the pre-class work and why their preparation will matter in class.

Students need to see the value of preparing for class with pre-class work. If they don't, they will quickly realize they can get by without doing it.

Reprinted from *Faculty Focus*, January 25, 2016.

Choosing an Approach for Small Group Work

by Claire Howell Major, PhD

Try the term "group work" in a Google search, and you'll find yourself bombarded with dozens of hits clustered around definitions of group work, benefits of group work, and educational theories underpinning group work. If you dig a little deeper into the links you return, however, you'll find that not all of the pages displayed under the moniker of "group work" describe the same thing. Instead, dozens of varieties of group learning appear. They all share the common feature of having students work together, but they have different philosophies, features, and approaches to the group task.

Does it matter what we call it? Maryellen Weimer asked this important question in her *Teaching Professor* article (2014) of the same title, with the implicit idea that one approach might be better suited for a given task than another. She believes that the answer to the question is yes. And she's right. As the adage goes, it is important to choose the right tool for the job at hand. A hammer is not the best tool for drilling a hole, and a drill is not the best tool for driving a nail. Both are good tools, when used for the appropriate job. So it is with group work. If you don't choose the best possible approach, then you will be less likely to accomplish the goals and objectives of the assignment.

While there are several different forms of group work, there are a few that are more often used than others and that have a body of research that supports their effectiveness. Three of these are cooperative learning, collaborative learning, and reciprocal peer teaching.

Cooperative learning

In this form of group learning, students work together in a small group

so that everyone participates on a collective task that has been clearly assigned (Cohen 1994, 3). A classic example of this approach is Think-Pair-
Share (Barkley, Major, and Cross 2014), in which the teacher assigns a
question, and then students think for a minute independently, form a pair
to discuss their answers, and share their answers with a larger group. The
goal is that all students achieve similar outcomes. Each student considers the
same teacher-assigned question, and they all work on performing the same
tasks: thinking, pairing, and sharing.

Collaborative learning

In this form of group learning, students and faculty work together to
create knowledge. The process should enrich and enlarge them (Matthews
1996, 101). An example of this form of group work is a collaborative
paper (Barkley, Major, and Cross 2014). In a collaborative group, students
work together to create a product that is greater than any individual might
achieve alone. They do not all necessarily do the same task, however, but
rather, may divide work among themselves according to interests and skills.
The goal is not for the same learning to occur, but rather that meaningful
learning occurs.

Reciprocal peer teaching

In this form of group learning, one student teaches others, who then
reciprocate in kind (Major, Harris, and Zakrajsek 2015). It is possible to
argue that this approach is a variation of either cooperative learning or collaborative learning, depending on the task. An example that leans more
toward cooperative learning is the Jigsaw, in which base groups study
together to become experts (Barkley, Major, and Cross 2014). The base
groups then split, and new groups are formed with a member of each base
group serving as an expert in particular area. An example that leans more
toward collaborative learning is microteaching, in which individual students
take turns teaching the full class (Major, Harris, and Zakrajsek 2015).

These three approaches are all tried and true group-learning varieties.
They all have been shown to benefit students on a number of outcomes,
from the acquisition of content knowledge to the development of higher
order thinking skills (Davidson and Major 2014). How is it possible, then,
to choose the right pedagogical tool for the learning task?

Pedagogical considerations

In choosing any approach to group learning, it is essential to start with
the learning goal. What should students be able to do after the completion

of the activity? If the goal is for them all to gain the same information, co-operative learning may be the best approach. If the goal is for them to create new knowledge, then collaborative learning may be the best approach. If it is to share knowledge, reciprocal peer teaching may be a good approach.

Learner considerations

When making any pedagogical consideration, it is essential to consider the students. Their level of expertise is important, for example, and if they are new to a subject and need foundational knowledge, then cooperative learning may be the best approach. If they are advanced students, then collaborative learning or reciprocal peer teaching may be more engaging for them.

Contextual considerations

While contextual considerations are not always the most glamorous, they certainly play a part in our ability to carry out group work. For example, if the class is a large one, a collaborative activity such as Think-Pair-Share may simply be more manageable than a long-term collaborative activity; likewise, reciprocal microteaching may be a great approach in an online class but would not be as feasible in a large lecture. A collaborative paper might be a great way to introduce graduate seminar students who work as research assistants at a flagship university to the process of co-authoring, but the same approach might not work as well for first-year students at a commuter college.

The intent here is not to prescribe a specific approach based on a tick-off list of considerations. Rather, it is to say that as teachers, we need to know what the instructional options are and to take into account the goals, the learners, and the learning context when making pedagogical decisions. Ultimately, we are in the best place to know what will work best in our unique situations, and it is thus our responsibility to choose well when deciding to use group work in the college classroom.

Reprinted from *Faculty Focus*, September 21, 2015.

Using Small Group Learning in the Flipped Classroom

by Claire Howell Major, PhD

When first deciding to flip your classroom, once you have decided to move content delivery outside of the classroom walls, a key question then becomes what to *do* with class time. Small group learning offers unique advantages for the flipped class. It draws on the principles of what we know about how students learn, namely by constructing knowledge. It also draws on strong pedagogical traditions, involving students in active, collaborative learning. It also helps students develop skills that are important not only to their success in higher education, but also to their future as employees, such as team work skills, emotional intelligence, global citizenship, communication skills, and leadership skills.

Finally, there is a solid base of research that indicates that small group learning improves learning outcomes, including foundational knowledge and higher order skills, retention and persistence, student satisfaction, and student comfort with diversity.

When using small group learning in the flipped classroom, consider some of the following questions:

How will you structure the group task?

For this issue, the goal is to be sure that the assignment relates to the course goals objectives, that the task matches students' skills, and that each phase of the activity is mapped out in advance.

How will you form groups?

Consider the size of the group (whether groups of 4–6 or smaller groups of 2–3), what the group member composition will be (will you have heterogeneous or homogenous groups), and how you will select group members (random selection or intentional selection).

How long will groups work together?

You may want groups to work together short term, such as for a simple pair discussion, long term, for example for a few class sessions, or for the entire term, as base groups.

How will you orient students to group work?

You may want to include information in your syllabus, use icebreakers to help students get to know each other, use team-building activities so that they learn group skills, and have students use group roles until they learn how to function as a group.

How will you facilitate group work?

You will want to consider your plans in advance, for example, will you introduce the activity? Observe groups? Will you interact with groups? How will you ensure closure?

How will you grade the groups' work?

Grading group work can be a challenge, so it is important to consider the question in advance. You can grade the individual product and the group product. You can have students complete self and peer evaluations as well. Using a combination of individual and group grades tends to be good practice.

There are many potential benefits to using group work in the college classroom, particularly in combination with a flipped classroom, and thinking through the key questions in advance means planning for success.

CHAPTER 2 REFLECTION AND DISCUSSION QUESTIONS

Use these questions for reflection, discussion, and application as you consider how to organize and plan successful flipped classroom learning experiences.

Reflection and Discussion:

1. Student preparation and motivation are the two most frequently discussed topics among faculty who flip their classes. What challenges do you anticipate as you introduce this approach to your students?
2. What strategies, processes, and ideas can you add to your classroom to address student preparation and motivation?
3. Many flipped classroom learning experiences are centered on group activities and discussion. What are some of the characteristics of successful groups and how you integrate these characteristics into the design of your course to ensure successful group learning experiences?

Application:

1. Review your lesson plan ideas from Chapter 1. Which of the learning outcomes, assignments, and activities lend themselves to individual versus group work? What types of group work do you think will be most effective for helping students achieve the learning outcomes?
2. As you consider your lesson plan from Chapter 1, what are some strategies you can use to both encourage students to come to the lesson prepared and ready to participate in the in-class activities you have planned?
3. What are some ways you might respond to students who come to this lesson unprepared? Thinking about it ahead of time can help you stay focused on your goal without taking away from class time.
4. If your lesson plan includes group work, brainstorm a few ideas for assessing groups. What is your purpose of putting students in groups? How much should the group work count as part of a student's final grade? Are you grading for both the process and the final product of working in groups?

CHAPTER 3
•
Connecting with and Reaching All Students

"As more faculty implement the flipped classroom model, new questions are emerging about how to design this type of classroom experience to work for all students. Some students will succeed in any learning environment regardless of the methods and teaching strategies we use. Some students thrive in these active learning classrooms. Other students are overwhelmed. Some students need more structure, and there are others who are more self-directed in their approach to learning. As we continue to study the flipped classroom model, it's important to consider all the different ways students learn so we can try to reach as many students as possible. Providing a variety of experiences in different formats also helps students build their mental dexterity, meaning their ability to learn in many different ways.

In the *Faculty Focus* reader survey on Flipped Classroom Trends (2015), many respondents indicated the flipped model increased student learning, engagement, and retention. Additionally, faculty are also beginning to share what students are learning beyond the content in the flipped classroom model. They see evidence of increased gains in students' transferable skills such as communication skills, leadership skills, problem-solving abilities, and the ability to work collaboratively.

In this chapter, the authors consider how we to connect with and reach as many of our students as possible using flipped and active learning classroom approaches.

"The Flipped Classroom: Tips for Integrating Moments of Reflection," encourages you to balance the activities with reflective strategies to encourage all students to process and organize their thoughts.

The second article, "Flipping Your Classroom Without Flipping Out Your Introverted Students," reminds us to design a flipped learning experience while keeping the needs of our introverted students in mind.

"Active Learning: Surmounting the Challenges in a Large Class" is not specific to the flipped classroom, but it addresses one of the challenges many faculty face as they consider how to actively engage 100, 200, 300 (or more) students.

Finally, "How Universal Design for Learning Supports the Flipped Classroom" combines the UDL principles with the flipped classroom model to create more opportunities to connect with and reach all of our students.

The Flipped Classroom: Tips for Integrating Moments of Reflection

by Barbi Honeycutt, PhD and Sarah Egan Warren

S tudents in inverted classrooms need to have more space to reflect on their learning activities so that they can make necessary connections to course content" (Strayer 2012).

If you were to observe a flipped classroom, what do you think it would look like? Maybe students are working in groups. Maybe each group is working on a different problem. Maybe the instructor is walking around the room talking with each group and checking on the students' progress. And each group of students is probably asking a different question each time the instructor walks by. It's probably noisy since everyone is talking to each other or engaged in a task. And students are probably standing up or leaning in toward one another to hear their group members talk about the next task. Students might be writing in a workbook, typing on their laptops, or watching a video on the screen of some new technological device.

The flipped classroom is a busy, collaborative, and social place. We could say it's a place where extraversion, collaboration, and teamwork are highly valued. But what does this mean for students who don't excel in this collaborative space? What does it mean if we're always focused on the doing? What does it mean for our introverts?

In the flipped classroom, the instructor's challenge is to design learning experiences that engage students in higher-level thinking and problem solving during class time. It's about creating, evaluating, synthesizing, and analyzing together. But, are we missing a whole segment of our student population and minimizing the importance of reflection in favor of active engagement by only defining the flip in terms of collaborative learning?

Other scholars have explored these questions from different

perspectives, all in an effort to learn more about how to increase student success, engagement, and learning. Felder and Silverman (1988) addressed it in their work with learning styles and learning preferences. Bonwell and Sutherland (1996) discussed it in their model based on the active learning continuum. Chesborough (1999) examined it in the context of the Myers-Briggs Personality Inventory (MBTI). Monahan (2013) suggests implementing strategies that allow both extroverted and introverted students to contribute meaningfully to the flipped classroom. It seems many of us are looking for ways to ensure all of our students are successful and feel valued in our classrooms.

There are numerous inventories and assessments for identifying how students' personalities, learning styles, and intelligences can inform the design of learning experiences. No matter your stance on these assessments, most of us are familiar with the language of extrovert and introvert. The MBTI, The Big Five, and the Strong-Campbell Interest Inventory all use this common vocabulary of extraversion and introversion. The vocabulary is the basis for the New York Times bestseller, *Quiet: The Power of Introverts in a World that Can't Stop Talking* (Cain 2012), and there are more than 1,200 books on Amazon dedicated to the introvert/extrovert terminology. The introvert/extrovert is a powerful way to think about the design of our learning environments.

So what does this mean for the flipped class?

Many flipped learning strategies seem to favor the extrovert (leading a class discussion, brainstorming as a group, engaging in small group conversations, playing games, creating models, recording a video, solving problems). All of these strategies require interacting, socializing, and working collaboratively. Students with a preference for extroversion get and expend their energy interacting outwardly and may feel more comfortable in these settings than their counterparts with a preference for introversion. While extroverts may thrive in these situations, drawbacks exist. As Cain (2012) explains, "The New Groupthink elevates teamwork above all else. It insists that creativity and intellectual achievement come from a gregarious place. It has many powerful advocates" (75).

However, are we missing valuable contributions from students who don't speak up or thrive in these highly interactive situations? Cain (2012) continues, "Introverts prefer to work independently, and solitude can be a catalyst to innovation" (74). Some of the best ideas may come from a student who worked on a creative task by himself/herself but didn't share it with his/her group. If we never give students an opportunity to reflect or work individually in the flipped space, then we're doing a disservice to both introverts and extroverts. <u>All students can benefit from reflection, not just introverts.</u> Reflection allows students time to pause, think, make connections, and work through an idea before others have any input or criticism.

If we refer back to the opening quote from Strayer (2012), the question we should be asking ourselves is, "How do we create the reflective space in the flipped learning environment?" Asking the question in this way puts this emphasis on the reflection, and reflection is a skill all learners need, especially in active learning environments and flipped classrooms. Asking the question in this way also encourages us to look carefully at how we design our time in class with our students. Simply moving all of the reflective activities outside of class time isn't addressing the needs of our students.

So, what can we do? To start the conversation, here are five strategies to integrate reflection into the flipped classroom:

1. Think, write, share

Similar to the popular "Think, Pair, Share" strategy many of us use in our classes, this strategy adds more time for individual work and reflection. Ask students to think about a question or problem first. After a few minutes, give students time to write, map, or draw their ideas. Then allow time for sharing in pairs, small groups, or among the whole class.

Example: In a technical writing class, ask students to individually identify the multiple audiences for a technical report and write 3–5 suggestions for improving the document design for the audience. Then share with a partner and contribute to a master list for the entire class.

2. Writing prompts

Begin class with a writing prompt based on the higher levels of Bloom's Taxonomy. Give students a chunk of time to create a draft, interpret a finding, or analyze two author's points of view, or analyze an idea at the beginning of class. Alternatively, if you assigned the writing prompt for homework, then allow students time in the beginning of class to re-read it and make edits before sharing.

Example: In a math class, ask students to compose a short paragraph (or a tweet) explaining how to apply a complex concept to everyday life.

3. SWOT analysis

Give each student a piece of paper (or access to a laptop or other technological tool). Ask students to conduct a SWOT analysis based on some part of the content. (A SWOT analysis is a method for identifying and analyzing the strengths, weaknesses, opportunities, and threats of an idea by creating a list for each of the four categories.) The lists in a SWOT analysis can be as detailed or as concise as your schedule allows. You could assign different students one category of the analysis if you have limited time.

Example: In a public speaking class, ask students to consider their own presentation skills in terms of their strengths and weakness and identify the opportunities and threats to developing better presentation skills.

4. Index card activities

Index cards can be simple yet effective tools to promote student reflection and engagement (Honeycutt 2016). You can design activities to give students time to reflect and think on their own before they engage in discussions and problem-solving within their small groups. And you can use the index cards to collect feedback and analyze student comments.

Example: Try the index card shuffle. To do this activity, give each student an index card. Ask them to write one question they have from the pre-class work or from the previous lesson. Give them time to think and review their notes. Then, collect all of the cards and put students into small groups. While they are forming groups, shuffle the deck of index cards and redistribute a stack of cards to each group. Ask the groups to distribute the stack of cards among their group members. Each group member reviews the question and writes his or her response on the back of the card. Then each student in each group can share the question and answer on their index card with their group members. Use this as a starting point for larger class discussions if needed.

5. Show and tell

Ask each student to bring a photo (hard copy or on a device) that symbolizes an idea or theory being discussed during class. Each student shares the image and explains the connection between the image and the concept. As an alternative, have students post the image to an online gallery, blog, or discussion board.

Example: In an education class, ask students to share a picture that represents his or her teaching philosophy.

By integrating moments of reflection into the flipped classroom, we can create a learning environment that both challenges and supports all learners and ultimately allow opportunities for all students to engage in both active and reflective experiences. We're not trying to change our students' ways of interacting with the world. As Monahan said, "Our goal is not to turn introverts into extroverts, or vice versa, but to maximize learning for all students."

When designing a flipped learning experience, use these types of activities to encourage students to think and reflect. These moments of reflection help *all* of our students succeed in classrooms where flipped and active learning strategies are used.

Reprinted from *Faculty Focus,* February 17, 2014.

Flipping Your Classroom without Flipping Out Your Introverted Students

by Nicki Monahan, MEd

One of the central features of a flipped classroom is the active learning that takes place within it. When students come to class having viewed a short lecture or read materials in advance, then classroom time can be devoted to engaging with that material, focusing on challenging elements, and applying what has been learned. This requires careful planning as the role of the faculty member shifts from being a transmitter of information to a designer of learning activities.

When designing learning activities for your flipped classroom, it is vital to keep the needs of all of your students in mind. Many extroverted students will be delighted to see the lecture hall transformed into a place where group brainstorming, problem-solving, and collaborative learning become the norm. For students who sit further along the introversion end of the temperament spectrum, the lecture hall perfectly suits their preferred style of learning. They may be less delighted at the prospect of change.

So, before you begin flipping, it might be helpful to consider the implications of temperament on teaching and learning. The concepts of introversion and extroversion, originally conceived by Carl Jung, have been helpful ways of understanding basic differences in human temperament (Jung 1970). Jung proposed that this critical element of our personality affects how we engage in social activity and influences our preferred levels of external stimulation. Extroverts prefer higher levels of stimulation and are typically are energized by social interaction, whereas introverts are comfortable with quiet and can find connecting with large groups of unfamiliar people exhausting. They may have excellent social skills and enjoy meaningful friendships, but are quite happy in their own company.

In an academic environment, introverts may prefer to work completely alone and discover their best ideas in solitude. They are typically quite comfortable in a lecture hall, listening and learning without the demands of engaging with others. If your flipped classroom involves constant group activity and a continuous buzz of students collaborating on projects, you may find your more introverted students voting with their feet.

In order to keep the learning preferences of all of your students in mind as you flip your classroom, consider these two planning principles: congruent choice and balance. The principle of congruent choice suggests that all students should have the opportunity, some of the time, to work and be assessed in ways that fit their temperament. For extroverts, who often understand what they are thinking by speaking out loud, and who thrive in social learning environments, this means that they should be able to work collaboratively, at least some of the time. For introverts, the opposite is true. They should be able to work independently, and in quieter environments, some of the time. In a flipped classroom, there need to be options with respect to active learning. Active learning does not require group work, all of the time. Students can be actively learning while having some quiet time to read a case study, review a spread sheet, write questions, or solve a problem. Balancing time provided to work together and to work independently, will respect the preferences of all of your learners, and will most likely produce optimal student performance as well.

When designing active learning strategies that involve collaboration in groups, it is also important to consider group size. More extroverted students may embrace "the more the merrier" attitude with respect to groups. Introverts, on the other hand, may be more comfortable working with a partner, or a group of three or four, rather than a larger group. When possible, and unless the task requires a large group for successful completion, consider providing options. A one size fits all approach may not be necessary and it certainly isn't preferable. You may assign a case study followed by questions, for example, with the instructions, "Work on your own, with a partner, or a small group. You have 20 minutes to prepare and then we'll discuss as a large group". Providing options demonstrates an awareness of your learners' differences and respect for different approaches to learning.

In a flipped classroom, there may be times when group work is the best way to actively engage with material that students have been introduced to outside of the classroom. And while it may not be the first choice of more introverted students, working successfully in groups is undoubtedly a twenty-first century job performance skill. Students should be required to take risks and stretch outside of their comfort zones. When assigning group work, however, it is important that the abilities of all group members are recognized and rewarded. In small group discussions, introverts typically prefer to listen first, gather their thoughts before they speak, and may be gifted in synthesizing the ideas communicated by others. In an effort to support introverted students, some faculty members have adopted the practice of assigning roles to group members. However, be wary of always assigning the introvert the role of group recorder; this can inadvertently communicate that their ideas are not a valuable part of the activity.

As Susan Cain suggests in *Quiet: The Power of Introverts in a World that Can't Stop Talking*, it's not always the biggest talkers who have the best ideas (Cain 2012). When students are encouraged to explore and discover the variable skills of group members, they may come to the realization that the "quieter" member who takes time to process before speaking has unique contributions to the group's efforts. Well-designed small group learning experiences draw on the skills of all group members rather than creating situations where the most extroverted and gregarious students control the learning.

When designing learning activities for your flipped classroom, consider the key elements of congruent choice and balance in order to create a comfortable learning environment for all your students.

Reprinted from *Faculty Focus*, October 28, 2013.

Active Learning: Surmounting the Challenges in a Large Class

by Maryellen Weimer, PhD

"Enabling interaction in a large class seems an insurmountable task." That's the observation of a group of faculty members in the math and physics department at the University of Queensland (Drinkwater et al. 2014). It's a feeling shared by many faculty committed to active learning who face classes enrolling 200 students or more. How can you get and keep students engaged in these large, often required courses that build knowledge foundations in our disciplines?

The article, *Managing Active Learning Processes in Large First Year Physics Classes: The Advantages of an Integrated Approach,* recounts how this faculty group did it in an introductory-level physics course required of most science majors at their university. They implemented an "integrated approach to active learning that supports the class activities with extensive preparation by both the teacher and the students. A key feature of our approach is the rich data it provides to teachers about student understanding before the start of each class" (Drinkwater et al. 77).

Their approach has two distinct phases: what the students do before they come to class and what happens during class. As with the flipped classroom model, these students are responsible for "covering" the content before they come to class. After completing the assigned reading, students take a short online quiz that must be completed 12 hours before class. The quiz questions are conceptual and interpretative (not problem solutions), which means the answers are written out. Students get full credit if they have answered all questions "seriously" (78) regardless of the number they have answered correctly. The team involved in the redesign of this course developed software that expedites the grading of the quizzes.

"Rather than the lecture being a teacher-led oration, the lecturer makes sure that any core concepts the students found difficult are discussed detail. . . . The focus of the class session is then a series of discussions of each of the core concepts for the lecture as defined by the learning goals for the unit of study, effectively turning the lecture into a mass tutorial experience" (78). This is why the teacher needs to be able to analyze student quiz answers quickly. Those answers set the agenda for what is discussed during the class period.

In class, "each discussion starts with one or more of the students' quiz responses [that] illustrate why the concept is difficult to them. The lecturer has the students work on a series of conceptual questions designed to build and test their understanding" (79). For each question, the students use clickers to answer individually, but they do not see the class response. Then they are encouraged to talk about their answer with those seated nearby, and after that they answer the question for a second time. This time they see the answers. At this point, the lecturer moves around the room with a microphone and asks students to explain why they chose a particular option, with the goal being to get multiple answers and perspectives. At the end of this exchange, the instructor reveals the right answer and summarizes the arguments that support it.

The team assessed the impact of their approach in a variety of ways. Physics is one of those fields that has developed standardized tests that can be used to measure knowledge before and after a first course. Two of these tests were used to measure learning gains in this study. For the Force Concept Inventory, the normalized gain for 154 students (in one course section) was 58 percent. Other research has established that the normalized gain in the same course taught in more traditional ways is 23 percent. In the second section, using the Brief Electricity and Magnetism Assessment, the normalized gain was 47 percent, which can be compared with 23 percent in traditional first-year university classes. Those are impressive gains.

The team also considered the effects of student engagement as measured by the clicker responses. The average percentage of correct answers when students responded individually was 55 percent. It jumped to 67 percent after students interacted with each other. A series of focus group interviews with students revealed an overall favorable response to the course design. The students noted how valuable it was when the majority of the class chose the incorrect answer to one of the conceptual questions, especially when they were confident they had answered it correctly. When they discovered they were wrong, as one student observed, "That's when I learn the most. That is revolutionary" (83). The standard course evaluation surveys also confirmed the positive response to this course redesign. "Our first unit was ranked among the highest first-year science courses for both overall student satisfaction, and for the amount of 'helpful feedback' received by students" (84).

The article continues with a discussion of faculty experiences preparing for and teaching the course. "It's a completely different activity when you walk into the room knowing exactly where students are in their own words—in a normal class you often don't find out until you make the final exam" (84). Teachers arrive in class knowing what students don't understand, what they misunderstand, and what is causing confusion. That said, the teachers in this project found that the approach required more preparation time. Some of this involved first-time-through issues like the generation of the conceptual questions used on the quizzes and in class. These could be reused, refined, or revised in subsequent classes. As might be suspected, it was also challenging for those faculty who were used to lecturing to talk less, giving students the time they needed to think and talk about the content.

"We cannot identify a single aspect of our approach that works above all others; it is the integration of all the practices into a coherent process that makes it such a powerful teaching and learning intervention" (86).

This article is noteworthy for another reason. It's the whole package—what exactly the faculty implemented (with references that support their design features), how they assessed the changes, what their results showed, and what they learned through the process. It's a remarkable piece of scholarship—it's both useful and readable!

Reprinted from *Faculty Focus,* April 22, 2016.

How Universal Design for Learning Supports the Flipped Classroom

by Thomas J. Tobin, PhD

The concept of Universal Design for Learning (UDL) was initially developed in order to provide equal access to learning opportunities for all students, regardless of how courses are offered or the challenges faced by learners. However, there is still a widespread perception that UDL is appropriate only for learners with disabilities. Faculty members are usually not clear about what UDL is, why it benefits students and instructors, and how to integrate UDL principles. Especially for designers and faculty members who want to flip their classroom interactions, UDL is a key approach that facilitates student engagement.

What is UDL?

Before we can address how to integrate UDL principles into our flipped classrooms, we should ground ourselves in a few core definitions. UDL began in the disability-advocacy community as a way of creating a more inclusive society, generally. "Recognition of disability as a civil right entails making sure that a person with a disability has access to the buildings, classrooms, and courts where those rights are learned and adjudicated" (Davidson 2006, 126). UDL is an outgrowth of universal-design ideas in the built environment—such as allocating parking spaces for drivers with disabilities.

The research scientists at the Center for Applied Special Technology (CAST) came up with the concept of UDL based on the various ways in which our brains process learning tasks:

"Universal design for learning (UDL) is one part of the overall movement toward universal design. . . . While providing access to information or to materials is often essential to learning, it is not sufficient. UDL requires that we not only design accessible information, but also an accessible pedagogy. . . . The framework for UDL is based in findings from cognitive neuroscience that tell us about the needs of individual learners. It embeds accessible pedagogy into three specific and central considerations in teaching: the means of representing information, the means for students' expression of knowledge, and the means of engagement in learning" (Rose et al. 2006).

We could see UDL through the lens of a medical model that perceives disability as a health issue, where disabilities are deficits that are inherent parts of individuals. This helps to explain why many people unconsciously associate negative emotions with their interactions with people who have disabilities (Stodden, Brown, and Roberts 2011): the "otherness" is associated with the people with whom we interact. Contrast this with a social model of disability, one in which disabling factors are in the environment. If a student in a wheelchair encounters a library building with no ramp, the disability is not part of the student—the disability is the poorly designed building itself. One way to move from the medical model to the social model is to think about designing the interactions in your flipped course for your learners who are using mobile devices like tablets and smartphones. How does UDL address "flippable moments"?

In the flipped classroom model, learners encounter new ideas outside of class time—and 85 percent of them today are using their smartphones to do so (Chen, Bennett, and Barber 2015). Students understand those new ideas best when they are presented in ways in which the learners take in information most smoothly. But how do professors and course designers know how each student learns best? Well, we don't. That's why UDL counsels us to present each piece of new information in more than one way: a "plus one" thought process.

With the flipped classroom model, it is best not to try to flip everything in a whole course. It's best to start by identifying "flippable moments" or places where active learning will add value to content mastery (Honeycutt 2013). Start by looking for places within the course where students are confused, bored, or where there's information they absolutely must know before moving on to the next part of the course. These moments are the places to invest the most time and energy in when flipping, and they can provide a good starting point for figuring out where to integrate UDL principles.

Imagine a single mother—call her Melissa—who is taking business management courses at her local community college. She has a job in order to be able to support her family, and she takes courses in the evenings and on weekends. She does her homework, engages with the course readings, and completes her course projects after 10:00 p.m., when the kids are finally in bed. Her statistics professor has posted video clips in the learning management system as study aids toward the midterm and final exams, but Melissa cannot take advantage of the videos because she doesn't want to wake her children and she doesn't want to tune her kids out all together by using headphones. Melissa does not have a disability, but she does have a challenge: time.

Now, imagine if Melissa's professor provided transcripts of the audio in the video clips, or, better yet, captions. Melissa can turn down the sound, turn on the captions, and study for her course examinations, while remaining available in case her children need her. Adopting good UDL practices lets Melissa's professor reach out to her—and to all of her classmates—with options that allows her to choose how she experiences the materials that the professor has posted. This is a double win: the professor's work in creating the videos, plus one alternative version, is rewarded with more students actually using the resources, and the professor's students are rewarded with more flexibility in how they study for the course and learn its materials, concepts, and processes.

Where should I focus my UDL efforts in my flipped course?

Does this mean that UDL requires us to create all possible alternative formats for our content? If that were the case, when we create videos of ourselves explaining course concepts, for example, we'd have to create captions, a separate text transcript, an audio-only version, and so on. If we think of how many separate files we want to create in order to support the class flip in the first place, having to make five times that number of files seem like an insurmountable obstacle.

But UDL doesn't work like that. It's all about providing learners with choices and control about how they move through the interactions in our courses. To maximize the utility of out-of-class content without multiplying the workload, ask three questions about the course content as it's taught in a traditional fashion:

- Which concepts do learners traditionally find challenging?
- Where do they always get things wrong on tests and assignments?
- Where do they benefit from different approaches to the content?

These "pain points" in the course are the focus points to start creating your "plus one" alternative versions of existing content files. Select one primary and one secondary format for all course materials. For most of us, our text-based course materials—that we already have—comprise our primary format, such as lecture notes, study guides, and practice quizzes, are the primary format. Then, by selecting a secondary format, such as audio-only, we are better able to do a whole course application of UDL within a narrowly defined scope.

UDL doesn't ask us to create materials to anticipate every possible use (e.g., students with visual disabilities, learners with poor Internet connections when they are going home on the bus), just to "design for the extremes," and add more ways of representing information later on, if and when new learner needs get expressed. CAST has created an Educator Worksheet to help professors and designers to work through this decision-making process (2011).

By offering instructional choices, students can select the learning pathways that work best for them—this is what differentiated instruction (DI) is all about (Livingston 2006). Just having more than one pathway through learning content and interactions opens up the benefits of differentiation; it is not necessary to plan for and execute every possible media approach in order to have a positive effect on student learning and persistence. A great place to start applying differentiated "plus one" design in the flipped classroom is with the use of media content. When you use videos to flip your classroom,

- consider alternative formats,
- integrate existing resources,
- segment them into smaller chunks, and
- design your videos to enhance or support specific learning outcomes.

This approach is more effective and engaging than recording every one-hour lecture for every class throughout the whole semester. The use of videos allows students to "pause and rewind the professor" (Ehlers 2014), but relying on videos alone to deliver the message does not address the needs of all learners.

Imagine a student on the football team at a large university in the southeastern United States: call him Jamaal. Jamaal is often on a bus or train, traveling to away games with his teammates. He already has a special arrangement that allows him to miss a certain number of in-person course meetings in his chemistry course, and he realizes that he's missing out on an opportunity for learning. He wants to keep up with his professor's narrated lecture slides, but his Internet connection is spotty when he is traveling. Jamaal has to wait until he is back on campus to be able to download and open his professor's PowerPoint slides from the course web-resources page, since his mobile phone doesn't have Microsoft Office on it. Jamaal does not have a disability, but he does have a challenge: resource availability.

Now, imagine if Jamaal's chemistry professor took the same narrated PowerPoint slides and created a screen-capture video version that the professor then uploaded to YouTube. Jamaal—and all of his classmates—could then stream the video, even under challenging bandwidth conditions, and he would not need any specific software title in order to experience the lecture slides.

How does UDL encourage active learning in the flipped classroom?

A final UDL strategy is to offer learners choices about how they demonstrate their skills. Many of us already know that it is a good idea to offer content to learners in more than way. The opposite is also true: when learners can choose how they show their knowledge, they tend to do better on assessments, projects, and quizzes.

For example, allow students to write a three-page essay or submit a four-minute audio or video clip. So long as the outcomes of the assignment are the same across all ways of doing it, you can grade an essay, an audio clip, and a video using the same criteria. A word of caution: If part of an assignment is the format itself (such as the margins, font attributes, and special sections of a business memo), then don't offer learners choices for those assignments—but do offer choices everywhere else.

Imagine a student—call her Amanda—whose National Guard unit is called up for an active-duty military tour of duty, right in the middle of her studies toward her nursing degree. Amanda's professor in her anatomy and physiology course requires all students to pass a two-part final examination in which the professor and student meet one-on-one and the professor quizzes the student in person on the names and locations of various parts of the human body. Amanda suspects that she will need to drop the course, since she will not be present to complete the final examination, and there are no options for demonstrating her knowledge in a different way. Amanda thought she could buy her own anatomical model, but a quick look online showed her that the model used by her professor costs more than six thousand dollars. Amanda does not have a disability, but she does have a challenge: distance.

Now, imagine that Amanda's professor offered students two different ways to take the final examination: in person (as above) or by Skype or other video-call software, using unlabeled diagrams provided by the professor ahead of time. The professor asks students to pan their cameras around themselves to show that there are no open books or study sheets being used; students can schedule the one-on-one time when and where it is most convenient to conduct the exam. Amanda uses the "private calls to home" area where she is deployed in order to do her live session for the final exam, and is able to continue her studies.

Conclusion

All of the examples in this chapter highlight professors adopting UDL techniques in order to reach out to their students who are using mobile devices in order to overcome distance, time, and resource limitations—challenges to which we can all relate. These stories about designing course interactions for mobile learners provide all of us with motivation to put in the effort up front to design experiences that intentionally enhance student engagement, increase learning, and decrease potential barriers.

To get started, follow these five best practices for implementing UDL into your flipped course design:

1. Start new design processes with text

You probably already have a text-based version of a lot of your course materials. Use it (or create it) as a "base layer" of materials that can support alternatives like audio and video.

2. Create alternatives for all multimedia

Remember that you don't have to create all alternatives—just one per element. Focus on creating alternatives first for the three "pain points" in your course where students have questions, get things wrong on tests, and ask for other explanations.

3. Design alternate ways for learners to demonstrate each course objective

This is a powerful approach. Give learners choices about how they show their skills, and they will tend to do better. Offer learners options like a written and spoken format, and be sure to use the same grading criteria and outcomes across all submission formats.

4. Break up tasks into separate components

Follow the mental rule of "ten and two." Give learners information for about ten minutes, and then ask them to take some action for at least two minutes. In the flipped classroom, it is especially important to chunk up content and ask learners to take regular breaks to perform application tasks like posting ideas to an online discussion, going on an Internet scavenger hunt to find resources, or just to take time with pen and paper for reflection about what they've just read.

5. Expand, document, and share interactions in online courses using free or low-cost tools

Like the example of the professor who converted narrated slideshows into movie clips to which any student could get access, you should determine which resources in your course require special software to see or use—and then convert them to more accessible formats.

Adapted from the Magna Online Seminar presentation, *Using Universal Design to Support All Online Students.*

CHAPTER 3 REFLECTION AND DISCUSSION QUESTIONS

Use these questions for reflection, discussion, and application as you consider how to organize and plan successful flipped classroom learning experiences.

Reflection and Discussion:
1. Why it is important to integrate reflective strategies into your flipped classroom?
2. What are some ways you can learn more about your students, how they process information, and how they learn best?
3. How can the principles of UDL enhance the flipped classroom?

Application:
1. Review your lesson plan ideas from Chapters 1 and 2. How are you designing the lesson to address a variety of learners? Where do you see opportunities to make changes or modify your approach to reach more students and connect them to the course material?
2. Choose one activity or assignment for this lesson. Brainstorm three different approaches or alternatives. Consider all the ways students learn and process information.
3. Choose one of the alternatives you brainstormed in question 2. Now outline it in more detail. What is the purpose? Where does it fit into the lesson? When and how will students complete it? How will you know they completed it? What tools or resources do you need to design this idea? What tools or resources will you need to provide for students? Plan the specifics.

CHAPTER 4

•

Assessing Learning in the Flipped Classroom

Many faculty struggle with how to assess learning in the flipped classroom. Do you focus on assessing the process? Do you focus on grading for mastery? Do you grade all the parts of the flipped learning experience: the pre-class work, the in-class work, and the post-class work? Does participation count toward the final grade, and if so, how does that work? How do you balance formative and summative assessments?

Because the flipped classroom is interactive and relies heavily on student engagement, collaboration, and experimentation, it is important to think about how to organize your assessment and evaluation strategies. One way to think about this in the flipped classroom is to make sure you're not only assessing learning, but also assessing how things are going. Don't be afraid to involve students in the assessment process, ask them about the activities, and make grading tools transparent so they know what to expect.

This chapter focuses on how to design assessment strategies to align with the flipped classroom model. The authors offer advice on how to stay organized, how to assess for different types of learning goals, and how to integrate assessment strategies into your course to determine how students are doing and what they are feeling.

The first article, titled "Four Strategies for Effective Assessment in a Flipped Learning Environment," features four strategies to support students at just the right time throughout the flipped learning experience.

"Assessment Strategies for Flipped Learning Experiences" encourages you to think about how you structure the pre-class assessment, in-class assessment, and post-class assessment in the flipped classroom.

In "Flipped Assessment," the author shares grading strategies, rubric development, and helpful tools. This article also includes a special "frequently asked questions" section about grading and the flipped classroom.

"How Universal Design for Learning Supports Concept Mastery in the Flipped Classroom" touches on how you can use the principles of UDL to think about assessment strategies for the flipped classroom.

"Ten Formative Classroom Assessment Strategies for the Flipped Classrooms" features ten different ways to assess students' learning so you can clarify key points, correct misunderstandings, and provide additional resources if needed.

Four Strategies for Effective Assessment in a Flipped Learning Environment

by Robert Talbert, PhD

Flipped learning environments offer unique opportunities for student learning as well as some unique challenges. By moving direct instruction from the class group space to the individual students' learning spaces, time and space are freed up for the class as a learning community to explore the most difficult concepts of the course. Likewise, because students are individually responsible for learning the basics of new material, they gain regular experience with employing self-regulated learning strategies they would not have in an "unflipped" environment.

But because initial engagement with new material is done independently as a preparation for class time, rather than as its focus, many things could go wrong. If students do the assigned pre-class work but don't acquire enough fluency with the basics—or if they simply don't do it at all—then the in-class experience could be somewhere between lethargic and disastrous. How can an instructor in a flipped learning environment avoid this and instead have consistently engaging and productive learning experiences for students in both the individual and group spaces?

A key to achieving this kind of environment is assessment. Because flipped learning is more decentralized and personalized than a traditional course, the challenge is to have assessments that provide reliable, actionable,and up-to-the-minute information about student learning in the various phases of flipped learning. Armed with this knowledge, instructors can provide just the right amount of support at just the right time, any time.

Here are four strategies for flipped learning assessment that can help provide this kind of support.

1. Start with good learning objectives.

The basic principle of backward design states that we should start by determining the learning outcomes we wish from students, then determine what constitutes acceptable evidence that students have attained these, and then design specific ways of gathering that evidence. Before any good assessment can happen, we need good learning goals. When designing a flipped course or unit, careful and clear enumeration of learning outcomes will give a framework for learning activities and help students know what they need to know, and where it fits in the overall scheme of the course.

2. Employ a "frequent and small" approach.

In an ideal world, there would be a device that connects directly into students' brains that would give a continuous stream of full-spectrum data about student learning and engagement. No such device exists yet, so the next best thing is to give assessments that are short, frequent, and informative and can collect these data for us. For example, classroom response systems can be used effectively to gather in-the-moment data about student learning. Short metacognitive activities, such as one-minute papers, can give a bigger picture. And don't forget that assessment doesn't necessarily mean quizzing or grading. Sometimes simply having students talk through a procedure while you observe them can give you mountains of "data" about how they are doing.

3. Use "pre-formative" assessment.

In addition to the usual categories of formative and summative assessments, flipped learning environments have a special third kind of assessment that I call "pre-formative." This refers to assessments given while students are learning new material independently, before any group interaction has taken place. Pre-formative assessment gives a reliable idea of what students have learned before the all-important group space activities you have planned.

Pre-formative assessments can serve not only as data-gathering opportunities, but also as learning experiences. For example, in the Guided Practice model of pre-class activities (Talbert 2014) students practice self-regulated learning strategies in acquiring fluency on new material while at the same time giving the instructor data about their attainment of basic learning objectives, in a format that is lightweight, risk-free, and welcoming to initial failures.

4. Act on, and share, the data you collect.

The purpose of assessment is to glean information that will improve student learning. When assessment data come in—from a reading assignment, a clicker question, a one-minute paper, and so on—ask: "What does it mean and how can this help?" In this way, the instructor takes on the role of resident data scientist in his or her class, converting data into information and communicating that information to his or her client (the student) with a view toward them attaining their goals.

It is helpful to remember that the word "assessment" comes from the Latin term meaning "to sit down beside." When we assess, it should be as if we are pulling up a chair next to each individual student, getting down on their level and putting ourselves in their corner to give them information that will help them succeed. In a flipped learning environment, the structure of the class puts students in a position to learn in improved ways, but it's assessment that opens the way to success.

Reprinted from *Faculty Focus*, August 10, 2015.

Assessment Strategies for Flipped Learning Experiences

by Robert Talbert, PhD

Successful flipped learning environments require that the instructor have knowledge of what students know and the items with which they are struggling at any point in time, and designing—and sometimes adjusting—learning activities to engage students where they are. This requires that intelligent assessment of student learning in a variety of contexts. These assessments take place in contexts that mirror the classroom itself: pre-class, in-class, and post-class.

Pre-class assessment

Pre-class formative assessment should focus on how well students are able to engage with new concepts in their individual spaces and should provide a safe space for students to encounter new concepts and practice them without fear of failure. A framework for this kind of assessment is provided by Guided Practice. Guided Practice assignments structure students' experience with new concepts in a single lesson within a specific framework that consists of:

- An overview of the lesson that gives the highlights of what is going to be learned, and how it connects to previous knowledge.
- Learning objectives, split into two lists: basic learning objectives stating what the student should be able to do before the class group space, and advanced learning objectives stating what the class will work on during the group space and what the individual will continue to learn following the group space.
- Resources for learning that include a mixture of media that provide raw material for learning the basic (and possibly advanced) objectives.

- Exercises that instantiate the learning objectives by giving students direct practice on the tasks in the basic learning objective list.
- A means of submitting the work that allows the instructor access to responses to the exercises prior to class, in order to make adjustments and have information about the class' collective understanding of the new topics.

In-class assessment

The in-class group space can be divided into three parts, with three distinct kinds of assessment:

- During the first five to ten minutes, students can be given assessments that hold them accountable for the pre-class work and give data on their understanding. These can include entrance quizzes over the basic learning objectives or key points from the readings and video, question-and-answer time in small groups, or randomly selected students presenting their solutions to pre-class work.
- The middle part of the group meeting is where most group time is concentrated. The entire point of flipped learning is to repurpose this time so students can work actively on difficult and engaging questions, hitting the upper parts of Bloom's Taxonomy. Activities that do this can include group problem solving sessions, debates, clicker questions that drive discussion, group writing or programming exercises, and more.
- During the final five to ten minutes, students can be given assessments that ask them to engage in metacognition and self-regulation, for example by having them write one-minute papers summarizing the work in the class; submitting their "muddiest points" from the class, or reflecting on their own personal understanding and feelings about the class.

Post-class assessment

Students can continue to work following the group space on the highest levels of Bloom's Taxonomy, where the activities for creating and analyzing sometimes require more time and space than the class group space provides. This time can also be used to further solidify student mastery on the lower-level objectives through more practice.

By planning and designing assessment activities throughout the learning experience, both you and the students can determine where additional information is needed to ensure the learning objectives are met.

Flipped Assessment

by Susan Spangler, PhD

For those of us who teach writing, especially in composition-rhetoric courses, grading and assessment takes a lot of time from our lives. It also can take a toll emotionally, as Nikki Caswell's (2014) work points out. And what do we get out of it? Students challenging the grades, administrators complaining about "too many 'A's" (or 'F's), hours of time spent reading and responding to student work, only to have students flip to the end of the paper to see the grade. What do students get out of it? A grade, a judgment of their work, and sometimes of them (or so they think), but not necessarily a learning experience.

Flipped pedagogy practices, however, have the potential to change the grading experience, just as they have changed traditional classroom dynamics. As it was articulated by Bergmann and Sams (2012), flipped instruction personalizes education by "redirecting attention away from the teacher and putting attention on the learner and learning" (11). As it has evolved, the idea of flipped instruction has moved beyond alternative information delivery to strategies for engaging students in higher-level learning outcomes. Instead of one-way communication, instructors use collaborative learning strategies and push passive students to become problem solvers by synthesizing information instead of merely receiving it. More recently, Honeycutt and Garrett (2013) have referred to the FLIP as Focusing on your Learners by Involving them in the Process of learning during class.

Flipped instruction changed the traditional, teacher-centered classroom in a lot of ways, with one major exception. Though the "centeredness" of classrooms changed to students, even in pedagogically progressive classrooms, assessment usually remains the sole domain of the teacher. As Belanoff (1991) explains, "[Grading is] the dirty thing we have to do in the dark of our own offices" (61). Assessment has been left out of the academic conversation and the scholarship on flipping, and though Honeycutt has developed assessments appropriate for flipped instruction, assessments practices themselves have not been flipped (Lorenzetti 2013). That is, students are typically not included in setting standards, responding to, or grading their work.

Why not?

If we want to involve students in their own learning as much as possible, let's flip assessment as well as the classroom to make assessment an integral part of teaching and learning. With this attitude, I decided to take flipped instruction one step further, to change the traditional form of assessment in my writing classes, to stop grading in the dark of my office. I set out to discover what happens when my students and I make the assessment process itself a learning opportunity. Though many instructors see assessment as a separate part of the learning cycle, a part that doesn't typically involve students, there are ways to shift the focus of assessment from the instructor to the student as well as to involve students in the process, thereby flipping assessment by making it a learning strategy. Here are a few ways I use flipped assessments:

Co-creation of rubrics

My students and I co-create course or assignment rubrics. This strategy allows students input on the standards by which they will be graded as well as a deeper understanding of what the standards mean. Instructors and students involved in the discussion during the co-creation of rubrics standardize their concept of quality work, giving students a clearer understanding of what they are being asked to do and the level at which they should be performing. Inclusion in the creation of rubrics also motivates students to participate more fully in the learning process.

In my classes, students articulate some if not all of the criteria by which they will be assessed. In some cases, we start constructing the rubric with the course goals as the objectives, and students articulate the different ways they might meet those objectives—how they could demonstrate that they have met them. In other courses, students have started from square one, determining the objectives for individual assignments themselves.

At a performance assessment workshop I participated in, I learned this about assessment: Students can hit any target that they can see and that doesn't move (Stiggins et al. 2004). Co-creating rubrics helps students see the target. By talking about the objectives for assessment, by negotiating the criteria, students see the target clearly and are active participants in learning. And when students who have input on the rubric also see the target clearly, they believe that the grading standards are clear and fair.

Reflection

Once students have articulated the rubric standards, I have students fill in their own evidence for meeting the criteria on their assignment/course rubric when they submit their papers. For the pedagogical theory on this, take a look at Kathleen Yancey's work, especially *Reflection in the Writing Classroom* (1998). When students reflect on their work, they come to understand that excellent quality is not an accident. The meta-knowledge gained during reflection makes the assessment a learning activity and not just a grading activity. Students show me in their reflections/analyses that they have learned something about the subject as well as the process of learning it.

In my courses, I give students a modified rubric with the articulation for the highest achievement level and then blank space for them to write in. This strategy enables students to reflect very specifically on their learning and to take an active role in the assessment process by directing my attention to their achievements. Instead of passively "receiving" a grade, students actively guide me in assessing their work in a particular context—one that they articulate. This method, coupled with the first, allows students to participate in authentic assessment situations that they might face in job performance assessments as current or future employees.

Grading with students

This unconventional strategy, much like flipped classrooms, actively engages students in learning during assessment. I've had colleagues say it can't be done. "They'd have to come in at 2:00 in the morning, because that's when I grade their papers," some professors have told me. Why do we wait until 2:00 in the morning to grade papers? Because we don't like to do it? Because we don't feel it's valuable to our students' learning? Making assessment a learning activity makes assessment valuable—both for me and for the students.

Having students sit with me while I grade takes the mystery out of how assignments are assessed, and it enables students to actively question, clarify, and understand why they are assigned their grades. That's called critical thinking. Their involvement in the grading process also allows me to see where students misunderstand points on the rubrics (where they're not "seeing" clearly) or in classroom instruction. Grading becomes a collaborative activity where learning by both instructor and student also takes place, unlike the one-way communication situation inherent in conventional grading situations.

I have students sign up for conferences, and when they come in, I pull up their documents on my computer (I don't look at the work before they come in, so if students want their grades, they have an incentive to come in as soon as possible after submission). I encourage them to take note of my comments because I don't write a lot and to ask clarifying questions they might have. I read their reflections and their work and then fill out the rubric, explaining why I mark each descriptor and where I am convinced (or not) by the evidence they have supplied in their reflections/analyses. I write one or two sentences on the rubric as a holistic reminder of what they did well or need to continue working on, and then I assign a grade.

I've been arguing that assessment should be part of a collaborative learning process, and I'd be quite hypocritical if I didn't share what I've learned from implementing these flipped assessment strategies.

During rubric co-creation, I've learned what students value in being graded, as well as some of the myths they have about what makes their work good. Sometimes during rubric creation, students want to use "tried hard" or "creativity" as a criterion. But because this is also a learning activity, we have an opportunity to talk as a class about what actually makes their work high-quality and how they might give evidence of it. I get to say why I can't always tell if they "tried hard" and that "creativity" doesn't always yield quality results. And then we negotiate a more specific criterion that all of us see clearly.

While reading students' reflections/analyses, I've learned that students don't always understand the language on rubrics or that they have a different interpretation than I do. As a result, I have changed rubric language to make descriptors more student-friendly, and I've changed my teaching habits to more regularly reference the rubric during class in an effort to help them understand the language. I've also learned where the weak points in my teaching are—what concepts need more explanation, practice, and focus in order to master.

By having students sit beside me while I grade, I've learned how to respond to students as a reader first, and I've learned to talk to them about their writing as separate from themselves. I think grading with students helps them separate themselves from the paper in this way: They have input on their grade, and they direct me to what they want me to look at, so their grade isn't just my judgment of them as students; it's really about their writing. Probably most significantly, grading with students has taught me the value of assessment. I no longer dread grading. I look forward to meeting with students and reading their papers, and I enjoy talking to them about their writing. I value the time I spend with them because I know they are learning from the experience, just as I am.

Students engaged in these flipped assessment strategies are reflective learners who generate evidence for their own assessments. They can take charge of how and why they learn, a major tenet of flipped instruction itself, or at least have a voice in that process. In this way, the energy of assessing their work shifts away from the instructor and toward the students, enhancing their learning in the process. Flipped assessment features a collaborative process where information flows between student and instructor instead of only one way. Finally, students are involved in the full process of learning, including the integral element of assessment, by their synthesis of standards and analysis of their own work. This is a powerful moment where pedagogy and personal/professional practices come together.

FAQs about flipped assessment strategies

What kind of technology is helpful for these flipped assessment strategies?
For rubric creation, I use a Google Doc that I project onto a screen as we fill in each criterion and description. If I have multiple sections of the same course, then I would share the Google Doc with all the students and have them edit and fill in their suggestions. We would have a virtual discussion on the document as well as face-to-face, course-section discussions to make sure everyone has the same understanding of the criteria and descriptors. I might also employ course-capture video or audio recordings so that students could listen to the discussions in the other sections instead of having their comments mediated solely by me.

For grading with students, I again use Google Docs with my students, who share their papers and reflections with me before the conference. When they come in for the conference, I open the documents on a big monitor hooked to my computer so we can both see the screen easily.

In order to schedule grading conferences, I share a weekly schedule with students via Google Docs so they can sign up for a conference time.

How much time does grading with students take?
Grading with students takes about the same amount of time as grading without them, just during the work day instead of after it. Instead of writing marginalia and a long end comment, I fill out the rubric and talk through most of the comments, writing down only the most important ones. I encourage students to take notes as I talk if they want to remember what I've said, and I encourage them to ask questions if they don't understand

something I've said or why I've marked the rubric in a certain way. Roughly, I spend 10–15 minutes with an individual student, depending on the assignment and paper length.

Do you apply this to all students in a class, or just those needing the most help?

So far I have applied grading with students to all of them in a course because I want them all to have the same experience. I have thought that in the future I might start by grading in front of students but later in the semester give them a choice if they want to continue this practice. It would be interesting to see if they would choose to come in on their own. I know I would prefer that they do.

I have enough trouble getting feedback to students without every class having a different rubric. How do you make this idea work on a 4/4 load?

If you are teaching the same course, then I would give students a skeleton of the rubric with the course goals already outlined and then let them fill in the gaps (if you're teaching a communal course, then the course objectives are probably already set for you). If you used a Google Doc, then everyone could have input from multiple sections of the course to create a common rubric.

If you're teaching different courses, then you would probably have different rubrics because you have different course goals. And of course you don't have to use all of these methods for every class. You might just start with having students reflect on their work and see how that flipped assessment strategy improves learning.

How have students responded to this assessment method?

The only drawback students have listed is scheduling time to meet, but by and large, the response has been positive. In course evaluations, students have reported that this course grading experience is more personal, important, and valued, and that they felt more confident in revising their work.

Reprinted from *Faculty Focus*, June 15, 2015.

How Universal Design for Learning Supports Concept Mastery in the Flipped Classroom

by Thomas J. Tobin, PhD

Universal Design for Learning (UDL) aims to gives all individuals equal opportunities to learn by creating interactions that work for everyone—not a single, one-size-fits-all solution, but rather flexible approaches that can be customized and adjusted for individual needs (CAST 2013). UDL helps with two aspects of the flipped classroom approach, specifically: 1) deep student engagement with first-exposure concepts, processes, and ideas; and 2) meaningful student expression during in-person group interactions.

UDL works best when learners receive feedback and encouragement about their progress in as close to real time as possible (CAST 2014). Especially since learners encounter new topics on their own, it's up to faculty members and course designers to structure the materials they are using in order to help keep learners engaged and interacting with the course concepts and with each other. This is one of the benefits of the flipped classroom model, as well. When students are engaging in activities and experiences during class, the instructor can immediately see their progress, identify areas of confusion, and provide resources and support to clarify misunderstanding and confusion. Students and instructors don't have to wait until a midterm or a final exam to make adjustments. This characteristic highlights the power of combining both the flipped model and UDL principles.

Because learners in the flipped classroom encounter new ideas outside of classroom-based or collective class time, it can be easy to misunderstand the flipped classroom model to require only that learners read the textbook or watch the lecture or review course materials during time spent on their own. Under such a misunderstanding we would thus expect students to master key concepts without any guidance from the instructor at all (Plotnikoff 2013).

Such a scenario is, in fact, identical to the old "chalk and talk" traditional classroom model where students study their notes on their own or prepare individually before in-class sessions. The flipped classroom model does ask learners to collaborate most closely and immediately when they are in the classroom together. However, not only does this not preclude the possibility of interaction and collaboration during out-of-class activities, but the level of learner engagement in out-of-class activities correlates strongly to how active they are as participants during in-class activities. Thinking about out-of-class interactions through the lens of UDL helps us to design activities that keep learners engaged, focused, and on task—even (perhaps, especially) when they are encountering new concepts and materials.

The importance of clear expectations

When it doesn't work well the first time, many instructors who try the flipped classroom model want to abandon it. In many such scenarios, neither the prof nor the students are clear about their roles and expectations. For example, if students are required to watch a video of a lecture, the instructor should say what they are supposed to do with that information. How do students know what information is important? How will they know what information will be applied during the upcoming in-person class session? This is why instructor presence and engagement are part of the out-of-class portion of the flip: We have to tell students explicitly what they should experience in their out-of-class encounters with new ideas. We have to be guides for their learning, even though we are not present to them in the classroom or via a live connection.

If instructors don't clearly design a path towards success, from the perspective of the novice, then students will disengage and resist. Students who are truly beginners may get lost without some structure and guidance, and more advanced students may feel that they are "going through the motions" of easier work. This ambiguity causes frustration and can lead to apathy, which can be interpreted by instructors as "it didn't seem to matter to the students." Students and faculty members may revert back to the more traditional roles of lecturing and taking notes during class time rather than engaging in the higher domains of critical thinking and analysis.

When writing directions for assignments, for instance, adopt a "cooking show" approach. Rather than list the steps for completing the assignment right away, talk to students about what they will accomplish, what the end result will look like, and what elements will earn points or credit for the assignment. Directions for assignments are also great places to include engagement messages from the instructor, like "In previous classes, students have said that this assignment is tricky; watch out for the shift in emphasis from earlier theories to later ones when you are creating your presentation," or "I am confident that you all have the core skills to do well with this assignment, and I want to give you permission up front to make changes to this assignment to meet your personal course goals. Email me if you want to make a change in your response to this assignment." Anything that allows learners to have a clear path and a sense of choice or control is both good universal design for learning and a good flipped class strategy for keeping learners on track and engaged outside of student-and-professor time.

Expressing concept mastery

This part of UDL for the flipped classroom model can be challenging to implement, but is also the most freeing for professors and students alike. Where possible, provide students with multiple ways to demonstrate their skills and learning. This does not necessarily mean having to create separate alternative assignments. Rather, look at the objectives for assignments and think of whether students must use a particular format in order to demonstrate those objectives, or if they can accomplish the same tasks in different ways. Also, figure out how much students need to do before they should take a moment to be reflective or take an action.

For example, break up tasks into information and engagement. Students might watch a five-minute video, read the first part of a textbook chapter for five minutes, and then take two minutes to reflect on the commonalities between the two resources. These reflection notes then feed forward into the next break for taking action, and create a foundation for richer in-class "flipped" conversation, as well.

Allowing learners to express their skills in multiple ways is often a new exercise for faculty members and course designers: if we ask learners to write a three-page essay, we can also allow them to choose to create an audio podcast or video report, so long as all of the alternatives provide students with the means to meet the required assignment objectives. Choice is a powerful motivational strategy. Not only is learner choice part of UDL, but it can be helpful in addressing some of the challenges of the flipped classroom model as well. Student motivation is often one of the top concerns for faculty members who flip their courses. If we can build in choice as an option for completing assignments, then we are addressing this challenge through the application of the principles of UDL.

For some assignments, such as learning how to write a business memo, the format is an integral part of the assignment; learners who created videos in response to such an assignment would not demonstrate good memo format. However, there are many kinds of assignments where the format is not integral to the skill set being demonstrated. In those situations, offer students the chance to create their responses to the assignment in any format that meets the objectives, or provide a list of possible formats, such as a written response, a short video report, an audio podcast, or a hand-drawn diagram that students then photograph and submit.

Not only does allowing multiple means of expression free up learners to select their best skill sets, but it also makes grading less of a repetitive chore. Many faculty members would rather see varied and creative responses to an assignment than have to grade dozens of five-page essays. However, if varied assignments are used, then the instructor needs to be prepared with several assessment strategies to accommodate the variety of assignments. This is not meant as a deterrent to inviting students to submit assignments in other formats. Actually, it can open up the potential for more feedback and less grading if designed carefully.

For example, one way to address this challenge is to integrate both formative and summative assessment processes. Formative assessments—such as classroom assessment techniques—are designed for practice and allow students to test their skills and knowledge and receive feedback without the high stakes involved in grading (Angelo and Cross 1993). Formative assessment tasks may be graded, but the percentage toward the overall course grade should be low. These "practice" assessments allow students to test their knowledge and correct their mistakes while giving the instructor valuable feedback about how to proceed, based on learner performance and feedback.

Formative assessment activities provide ideal opportunities to try alternative assignment formats. In the business memo example, a flipped strategy would be for students to write a summary or record a one-minute video explaining in their own words how a memo is formatted and why it matters. Or, in another flipped strategy, students could be given a poorly formatted memo and asked to correct it by circling the errors and explaining how to make corrections. These activities would be completed during class time to allow students to practice analyzing, evaluating, and creating skills before they are given a summative evaluation such as a test, project, or final exam where the students would demonstrate mastery.

Conclusion

Here are some summary ideas about using UDL to foster concept mastery in a flipped class:

- **Look at interactions in the course from the perspective of a novice learner.** Don't just think like a beginning in the subject matter, but also think like a beginner who is using the tools or techniques, as well. Just writing "I know that the flipped classroom might be new to you; here are some hints about what to do when you read these articles" helps students to feel that it's okay not to be an expert at the mores and rules of the space in which they are interacting.

- **Set clear expectations for both learners and instructor behavior.** Faculty members and developers are typically very good at telling students what to do, and when, and how many points it will be worth. We can be less forthcoming about our own behaviors. Student anxiety and uncertainty goes way down when we tell them, for instance, how long they should expect to wait for a response during out-of-class communication sessions—and put that note right into the discussion forum or communication venue so they will see it when and where they need to see it.

- **Build in choices and paths for the interactions in the course.** Especially for moments when students encounter new ideas on their own, make sure they are not completely alone. Put in explanatory and encouraging notes from the instructor, video snippets with advice and ideas about how the student should approach and think about the content—anything that increases the instructor's presence for students while they are moving through content and interactions on their own. Offer them choices, too, about how they demonstrate their skills, especially on projects and tests.

By introducing multiple ways for students to demonstrate mastery and test their knowledge, your students will become more engaged and prepared for their in-person class time. And by modeling different approaches and formats to the students, you can motivate your students to do the same when they complete their assignments.

Ten Formative Assessment Strategies for Flipped Learning Environments

by Barbi Honeycutt, PhD

By design, flipped and active learning environments encourage continuous opportunities to assess students' learning. When you're walking around the classroom talking with students listening to their conversations and providing support when they ask questions, you're engaging in formative assessment. I like to call the flipped classroom "assessment in action" because you—and your students—are constantly testing an idea, seeing if it works, retesting if necessary, and determining where "gaps" in understanding are. Maybe that's why it's hard. And maybe that's also why it works.

Formative assessment is a way of informally gathering feedback about students' learning. Formative assessment allows you the opportunity to check in on your students so you can provide additional support or resources if needed. Typically, this type of assessment is not graded, but it is collected or reviewed to determine what sticks and what doesn't. You can certainly attach a participation grade to formative assessments if needed, but just remember that the whole purpose of formative assessments is to give students a chance to practice.

There are literally hundreds of formative assessment strategies, also called "classroom assessment techniques," and you can use them at any moment during class (Angelo and Cross 1993). You could use one of these assessments as a focusing activity during the first few minutes after class begins (Honeycutt 2016b). You could try one in the middle of class to help students regroup or re-energize (Honeycutt 2012). Or, you could add one to the end of class to determine which topics need more discussion or explanation.

Here are ten formative assessment strategies to help you get started:

1. Your one-sentence summary

Ask students to write a one sentence summary in their own words. A few examples: (1) Summarize a theory; (2) Interpret the first four lines of a poem; (3) Explain the final answer to a problem; (4) Explain the main point of the video; (5) Justify a decision based on the findings presented in an article.

2. Ticket out the door

Plan 2–3 minutes at the end of class for students to write, solve, fill in the blank, or plan the next step of their research project. After they fill in their response on a sheet of paper or index card, they must submit them to you before leaving class that day. Alternative: Try using a ticket in the door to get students to come to class prepared.

3. Three things I learned

Ask students to write three things they learned in class. This strategy is interesting because it will allow you to see what types of activities and topics create the most interest. Do students only remember what was covered during the first few minutes of class? Do they mainly remember the activity or demonstration you used? Did they get the main point of the video?

4. Clearest point, muddiest point

Here's a popular classroom assessment technique from Angelo and Cross (1993). At any point during class, most likely at the end, ask students to write one concept they clearly understand or remember from today's class (clearest point). Then, ask students to write one concept that is still confusing or something they are uncertain about (muddiest point). When you review their responses, you will most likely see themes emerge in terms of what sticks and what doesn't when it comes to the types of teaching and learning strategies you used in class. It also boosts students' confidence because they can explain what they know while also allowing them the opportunity to ask for additional clarification about something that is still causing confusion.

5. The one takeaway

After an experiential activity, discussion, or mini-lecture, give students time to write the one concept they took away from the experience. What's the big lesson they learned? What do they remember? This can be written as a reflective blog post or journal entry, or students might post it on a discussion board so they can share their ideas with their colleagues.

6. Draw it

Looking for a creative alternative to assessment? Give your students a blank sheet of paper and ask them to draw a concept from the lesson. If you have enough time, students can share and discuss their drawings in small groups and teach their interpretation of the concept to their peers. You can also adapt this idea and ask students to draw how they study, how they write a paper, or how they prepare for class.

7. Explain it to a 7-year-old

Ask students to explain a complicated course concept as if they were teaching it to a child. The point of this exercise is to help students focus on the "why" and the "how" instead of getting too overwhelmed in all of the technical jargon.

8. One-minute paper

Another popular classroom assessment technique from Angelo and Cross (1993) is the one-minute paper. Give students one minute to write about a concept from class, from the video, or from the reading. In one minute, they should be able to convey the main point. If not, this exercise will help them focus, refine, and condense their message since they only have one minute to respond.

9. One more question

No matter how much time we allow for questions, it seems there's always one more question someone didn't have time to ask. Here's their chance. At the end of class or before the next class, ask students to write one remaining question on an index card. Then you can review these for continued discussion, or you can distribute the index cards randomly in the next class and see if other students can answer the question written on the card. You could also adapt this technique for a homework assignment or group activity.

10. What's next?

If you've reached the end of a unit or module, or if your students are preparing for a test or project, take a moment to help them articulate the next step in the process. Give them a couple of minutes to organize their thoughts and write their plan for the very next step they need to accomplish before they can move ahead. If you decide to review this information, it'll show you where your students are in a process and it could help students avoid procrastinating.

These ten formative assessment strategies are designed to give your students an opportunity to practice and reflect, and they give you an opportunity to get feedback without waiting until the final exam is prepared or the final project is due. Try combining a couple of these together, and use them during random moments during class and throughout the semester. Be careful not to overuse them or do the same one too often. Mix it up—if you use the same one all of the time, they will lose their effectiveness. If students know the assessment is coming, then the point of the activity will be diminished.

Examples of assessment planning tools and mapping grids are included in the back of this book.

Adapted from the Magna Online Seminar presentation, *Assessment Strategies for the Flipped Classroom.*

CHAPTER 4 REFLECTION AND DISCUSSION QUESTIONS

Use these questions for reflection, discussion, and application as you consider how to organize and plan successful flipped classroom learning experiences.

Reflection and Discussion:
1. Why is it important to begin with well-written learning outcomes? How do you know if your outcomes are clear, specific, and measurable? What resource(s) do you use to help you create learning outcomes?
2. What is the difference between formative and summative evaluation? How do you integrate both into your courses? How will you (or how do you already) plan for both of these approach in your flipped classroom?
3. How does UDL help both instructors and students when planning assessment activities in the flipped classroom?

Application:
1. As you continue refining the lesson you'd like to flip, go back and review your learning outcomes. Are they specific and measurable? Can you map these learning outcomes to specific pre-class assignments, in-class activities, and post-class tasks? Revise as needed.
2. Plan an assessment activity for your flipped lesson. Consider a classroom assessment technique, a formative assessment strategy, or another way for students to practice and receive feedback.
3. As you think about summative evaluation assignments, what are other formats or ways students could demonstrate concept mastery in this lesson? What are the assignment goals? What are the specific tasks? Will you use a rubric? How will you (and the students) know the learning outcomes have been met? Brainstorm these ideas and then choose two different approaches to plan in more detail.

CHAPTER 5

•

Integrating Technology into the Flipped Classroom

In the *Faculty Focus* Flipped Classroom Trends reader survey, more than 80 percent of the respondents indicated they feel students are comfortable with technology as part of the flipped classroom model (2015). Although it's not a requirement to flip a class, many faculty integrate technology into their flipped classroom to enhance the learning experience. Students may watch videos, listen to podcasts, discuss ideas in online forums, connect on social media, and use collaborative learning tools to work in groups.

The three-part structure of the flipped classroom usually includes: (1) pre-class work where students connect with the course content; (2) in-class work where students apply and analyze the content, often collaboratively with others; and (3) post-class assignments to follow up, assess learning, and connect to the content to prepare for the next part of the lesson. Technology may be integrated into any one—or all—of these structures. This means there are many ways to think about the role technology can play in the flipped classroom model.

But, how do you know what types of technological tools to integrate? How can you make the online learning experience as engaging as the in-person learning experience? How can you use these tools in innovative and dynamic ways to enhance student learning? In this chapter, you will be introduced to a variety of ideas to help you integrate technology into your flipped classroom.

"Broadening Student Learning with Laptops" examines how laptops can be integrated into the flipped classroom to enhance student learning

"Five Ways to Flip Your Class Using Discussion Boards" shares five flipped strategies to enhance student engagement in the online portion of your class using discussion boards.

"Flipping the Feedback: 'Screencasting' Written Feedback on Student Essays" presents an alternative way to use technological tools to provide feedback to students.

Finally, "Can You Flip an Online Class? Seven Flipped Strategies to Enhance Engagement" presents ways to engage students in the online environment using the flipped learning model.

Broadening Student Learning with Laptops

by Sarah Gaby and Howard E. Aldrich, PhD

Calls to ban laptops in college classrooms are based on accumulating research showing their negative effects not only on users but also students sitting nearby (Sana, Weston, and Cepeda 2013; Fried 2006). Just a few students on their laptops in a classroom have the potential to disrupt the concentration of all the others in the room. Research indicates that while students share the belief that they can simultaneously pay attention to what is happening in the classroom while surfing the web, checking emails, looking at course-related materials, and visiting social media sites, cognitive neuroscientists find otherwise. Most of the negative press on laptop use appears to stem from the use of laptops in large lecture halls and in classrooms where Internet-connected laptops are serving little or no pedagogical function. Despite these negative perceptions, we feel that laptops do have a place in classrooms. We believe that strategic use of laptops integrated into classrooms can enhance both student learning and instruction.

We acknowledge the problems laptops can cause, as studies of laptop use in the classroom have documented their potentially detrimental effects on learning. Students who use laptops are found to multitask, detracting from their attention to the course as well as that of their peers (Sana, Weston, and Cepeda 2013). Students who utilize laptops report reductions in learning, understanding, and performance compared to those of non-laptop using peers (Fried 2006). These negative outcomes not only result from students using laptops to browse non-course related content, but also occur when students simultaneously engage with course material on their laptops during lectures (Hembrooke and Gay 2003).

But, do the problems stem from the physical presence of the laptops or from instructors' neglect of the pedagogical potential sitting on students' desks? Based on our experiences and those of our colleagues, we believe that the pedagogical payoff for instructor-guided laptop use far exceeds the potential for misuse. While findings critical of using laptops in the classroom have led many teachers to ban laptops, other findings emphasize the importance of laptops and mobile devices as innovative technologies that have changed the available toolkit for teaching and learning (Bransford, Brown, and Cocking 2002). Instead of asking whether computers are beneficial or disruptive in classrooms, instructors should ask, "In what ways can technology bolster my teaching goals and objectives?"

In this article, we suggest several ways that technology might enhance the classroom experience for both teachers and students. We draw on existing research and our own approaches to technology in teaching to develop these ideas. They are by no means an exhaustive list of the potential ways flipped classrooms can be enhanced, but we hope they will offer guidance and help you innovate within your own realm.

First, technologies can be used in classrooms to level out the knowledge base. Students come into classrooms with vast differences in knowledge and interest. In the commonly used model of an instructor-led classroom, instructors must determine how much students already know about a topic, either from previous classes or assigned readings. They then use this understanding to determine the level at which to pitch their lessons. As an alternative model, try using brief and predetermined amounts of class time on laptops and other devices to let students explore topics in class, based on their own knowledge base. For instance, at the start of class, students may be asked about a topic related to the one being discussed and directed to find the answer using their laptops. The activity can be done in groups as well, allowing the more technologically sophisticated students to take leadership roles.

Second, real-time problem solving in classrooms is enhanced by technology. Often during class discussion, problems will arise that cannot be answered through the assigned readings. For instance, when discussing a social movement, students might wonder what sorts of "free spaces" Civil Rights movement participants utilized. Instead of instructors providing answers, laptops and smartphones allow students to find the answer on their own. This approach empowers students to learn for themselves, rather than relying on the instructor, thus reinforcing metacognitive strategies students can use outside the classroom.

Third, technologically enhanced learning strategies can expand opportunities for feedback, evaluation, and self-reflection. Students can use online programs to take short quizzes on course information, evaluate their success in answering, and look up more information on missed answers. Techno-logical programs often model metacognitive learning processes, asking that students evaluate their progress and play an active role in their own learning (Bransford, Brown, and Cocking 2002). Students can use short surveys to provide information on course material, feedback to teachers about their teaching, and reports of their interest in the topic.

Large lecture classrooms have been cited as a problematic venue for flipped classroom activities. However, with appropriate tools, laptops and smartphones that instantaneously collect and display data can be used to quickly engage students. For example, programs such as Poll Everywhere invite students to use their devices to answer questions posed during class, displaying the answers on the classroom screen for instant analysis. Teachers can thus immediately see whether students understand a concept and re-spond accordingly in real time. They may also be useful for collecting opin-ions on a topic, quizzing students and anonymously displaying aggregate answers, and taking attendance.

Fourth, technological devices can be used as a tool for class activities. In a flipped classroom environment, students often use their laptops to solve problems, review video lectures, and respond to pop quizzes produc-ing immediate results that can be used inside the classroom (Fulton 2012). Whole class collaboration becomes possible with the use of technological innovations that allow everyone to simultaneously access and work in the same digital space. For instance, in one activity, students may be asked to design a poster in support of a particular political viewpoint. By using their computers to respond to this class activity, they can look at samples of simi-lar posters, collect data and information needed for the project, and quickly produce a product that can be displayed for classmates to view.

Fifth, technological devices can aid student-led teaching efforts by help-ing students develop, lead, and gain comfort taking on great responsibility in class. We often ask our students to lead activities or teach topics, and laptops provide a mechanism for gathering information, sharing video clips, relevant photos, and other information as well as a medium students find comfortably familiar for presenting to their class.

Finally, critics argue that laptops on desks in front of students disrupt student-teacher face-to-face contact. In fact, laptops can help instructors stay engaged with students. Moving around the classroom while students are using their computers for individual research or group work connects professors to students and provides occasions for less formal interac-tions. Staying connected to the students rather than standing behind a podium, we suspect, greatly reduces the chances that students will make non-instructional use of their laptops. Nonetheless, we encourage instructors to say "close your laptops" or limit their presence in other ways when they're not being used for learning activities and exercises.

The lessons we draw from these examples is that to be truly beneficial, laptop use must be crafted to meet the needs of specific courses. Instructors who successfully utilize technology in their courses can improve both their teaching and student learning. Whether or not laptops are a part of your classroom, we hope these ideas will spark new ways to use these tools to engage your students.

Reprinted from *The Teaching Professor* newsletter, April 2015.

Five Ways to Flip Your Class Using Discussion Boards

by Stephanie Delaney, JD, PhD

In a flipped class, the discussion board gives you a great way to engage in conversation outside of the face-to-face classroom. However, it can easily be used as a crutch to have something, anything, for the students to actually do when they are online. Yet, keep in mind that many, if not most discussions are better in a face-to-face environment. They are more fluid, more immediate, and more natural for most students. Thus, when considering using discussion boards in your flipped classroom, you need to have a good reason to do so.

One great reason for online discussion when face-to-face discussions are also an option is that many students don't participate in face-to-face discussions. There are often just a few students who dominate the conversation, while a few others chime in. In any discussion, a third or more students might not participate at all. The slowed conversation that happens as a result of asynchronous conversation has several advantages for students that you might not hear from in face-to-face classroom:

- Second language learners have time to correct their work so they feel comfortable expressing themselves when they might not in the face to face classroom
- Perfectionists who like to have an argument completely formulated before they express it
- Shy students who don't like to call attention to themselves in a conversation

Once you have a good reason to use the discussion forum, remember these simple tips to keep your discussions lively and relevant:

Each question should have infinite answers.

Adult education pedagogy recognizes that adult learners like to contextualize their learning, making it relevant to their lives. When students are able to do that, they are more likely to engage in the work.

One of the easiest ways to create a space for that kind of contextualized learning in a discussion board is to create questions with infinite answers. This would be a question that, for example, relates to a student's live experience. Here is an example:

One answer: Describe how a bill becomes a law.

Infinite answers: Find a law that impacts your life and describe how it moved from being a bill to being a law. How is your life different now that the law is in place?

In general, finding a way to personalize the question will make it have infinite answers, depending on the life experiences of your students. It also makes it much easier for students to find something interesting to respond to when engaging in the discussion.

There are course topics where personalizing the learning is not going to work, but in those cases the discussion topic can encourage a sharing of observations on how the students have learned or struggled with that week's work.

Make the credit reflect the value.

It is important to create a value for your discussions and grant that value to the students. If it is really important to you that students participate in discussions, then they should earn a significant portion of the week's points for engaging in the activity.

Some instructors in flipped classes don't want to give credit for engaging in online discussion if they don't also give credit for discussion in class. While there is some logic to that, if you don't give credit for the discussion, many students simply won't do it. Perhaps the better way to be fair is to give credit for classroom discussion rather than not give credit for the online discussion. Another option is to give a single discussion grade for each week/module/unit which incorporates both online and in class participation. Be sure to create credit options for students who are reluctant to speak up in the classroom.

You'll also want to be clear about how the discussion is graded by using a detailed rubric. If possible, include a variety of examples of good and not so good discussion responses with commentary, so that students really know what a good response looks like. If you are new to online discussions, you can achieve the same end by highlighting one or two student posts each week and describing what elements made them quality posts. As the term goes by, you'll see the quality of posts improving. In creating the rubrics, you don't need to recreate the wheel. Borrow from your peers and others that have gone before you.

There should be multiple due dates.

An asynchronous discussion ideally spans over some period of days, giving students time to have some back and forth in the discussion forum conversation. While your top students may do this naturally, most students tend to wait until the deadline to do the work. If you have one due date, the students will wait until that last day and do all of their posts and you will not have a genuinely fluid discussion happening.

One option is to have two due dates, one for the initial post and one for replies. That way, your early birds have something to respond to and your last minute folks still get the benefit of responses to their main posts.

You might also encourage more frequent participation by having students post on multiple days during the discussion period, separate from the due dates. For example, you might have two due dates, but require students to post on three separate days. Again, this gives students a chance to see who has responded to them and to more fluidly participate in the discussion.

Note: If your learning management system only allows one due date, you could set the due date as the main post due date and the reply date in your LMS calendar as an event.

Five ways to flip

Once you've devised your strategy for most effectively using discussion boards, it's time to create some assignments that flip the classroom using discussion boards. Here are five ideas to get you started.

1. Group work

Group work can be a great way to encourage student learning and online discussions can really help groups engage. You could have groups work on research projects, have lab students create a procedure checklist together or have language learners create a second language summary of an article of current news event. You have to be strategic, though, when using discussion boards with groups.

In most situations, you would ideally begin group work in the classroom. Groups gel more quickly and easily when you give your groups a chance to form and get to know each other in the face-to-face environment. Depending on the maturity and motivation of the students, you might want to use the discussion boards only for keeping in touch between face-to-face class sessions rather than doing substantive work.

The most important key to a successful group project, particularly in a flipped classroom, is crystal clear instructions. To effectively use discussion boards as support for the group work, you need to provide a lot of structure. There are many suggestions available on the internet on effectively doing group work online. To get started, you'll want to consider the following:

- Very detailed instructions—What exactly do you expect students to do using the discussion board? Collect and share research? Work on drafts? Substantively create the final project? Be really clear in order to avoid frustration—the student's and your own.
- Assign roles—One way to provide structure is to assign roles or to give a set of roles and have the students use them as a starting point for creating their own structure. Roles include researcher, devil's advocate, cheerleader, summarizer, etc. You can easily find suggestions for group roles by searching "roles for group work" in your favorite search engine.
- Consider two-way grading—One thing that stresses students out about group work is the possibility that their grade rests on the work of others. To avoid potential problems, perfectionist students feel they have to do all of the work while slacker students are easily able to avoid doing anything. Work around this with two-way grading—giving both a group grade and individual grade. You can have each student grade the members of the group as well as their own contributions and use that for creating the individual grade. Students are remarkably honest about this kind of grading. It creates a needed accountability while relieving stress.
- Rubrics—Identifying exactly how students will be graded using a rubric is another practice that will reduce students stress and increase your grading effectiveness. Talk to peers or search the internet for "group project rubric."

2. Peer polling

One fun way to have students engage is by sharing their learning with friends and family. They can do this using informal peer polling. In peer polling, you have students ask their friends and family a question related to the course and then collect their responses to the questions. The students then share their findings on the discussion board and reflect on the results.

For example, in an American government class you might have students ask, "What are your First Amendment rights?" In order to effectively poll friends and family, the student must first know all of the First Amendment rights. They also need to be able to explain them, particularly the ones that people are least likely to remember like the right of assembly. If you ask them to poll 10 friends, they end up engaging in 10 different discussions about the First Amendment. The students have the added benefit of discovering, depending on their circle of friends, how little people really know about the constitution.

This activity works well in almost any discipline. For example, you might have students poll friends and family about how to determine the circumference of a circle, whether they can identify the chemical formula for air, or whether they know any Italian words that have nothing to do with food.

Be clear in instructing students how to share the results on the discussion board. Do you want individual responses or should the student compile the results? Should they also share a little about the group of people polled and how they were polled (in person, using Facebook, etc.). You might also have students discuss the results of their polls in small groups in class and then have the group post the compiled results and their observations and build a discussion around that.

3. Community interviews

Another great way to engage students and flip the classroom is to have students do community interviews. Have students find (or the instructor can provide a list of) people in the community who can speak to issues related to the course. For example, in an American government class, students spoke to members of their city councils, the park and school boards, etc. to ask them about community service. The students then crafted their interview into a discussion post and shared with the class.

Community interviews could be used in nearly any discipline. Try, for example:

- Interviewing local government employees about environmental regulatory enforcement
- Interviewing local elected officials about voting
- Interviewing church and community leaders about ethical issues related to health care
- Interviewing college leadership about what goes into cost of college for economics

There are many different things that students could do with the results of the interviews beyond posting to the discussion board. They could create a short documentary alone or in a group. They could do small group sharing about the interviews in class and report out to class on a larger discussion board.

Encourage students to record the interviews using audio or video. They can use tools in your LMS mobile app or built-in camera tools in their mobile devices. Students can then (optionally) post short audio or video clips of their interviews. Some faculty are wary about asking students to record because they are not fully comfortable doing it themselves and don't know how to give instructions. You'll find that many students can easily do this on their own and are willing to help other students who need it. Just be sure to give students time to collaborate. You can also seek help from the media services or eLearning departments on your campus and let them provide any technical instruction and support.

4. Field trip

Most courses have real-world applications. Have students explore some of them with a field trip. Students can prepare an audio or video presentation and post it on the discussion board as a prompt for class discussion.

Again, you'll want to be clear with the instructions that you give the students about this assignment. Give the students some guidance about what should be explored—local museum, public meeting, fish-bearing streams, the office of a professional working in the field. Give them guidance about the goal of the field trip so that the posts can be focused. It is also helpful to give guidance on the length of the post—three to four minutes is usually sufficient and is as much as other students (and you) would be willing to watch.

As noted in the community interviews section, there is no need to worry about instructing the students on how to do the field trip recordings. Give the students the opportunity to teach each other and/or solicit the assistance of your media services or eLearning departments. You can focus on your subject matter expertise and capitalize on the technical expertise of others. Even if you are very savvy with recording technology, this division of labor frees you up from being tech support for the project and sends it to the actual help desk, where it belongs.

5. Movie night

Another fun way to engage students outside of the classroom is to have a movie night with friends and family, watching an assigned movie related to the class. For example, in an environmental studies class students might watch "An Inconvenient Truth" or in a legal ethics class they might watch "The Firm." You might provide discussion questions or have them develop their own individually or in groups—using the discussion board.

After watching and discussing the movie, students can share their reflections on the discussion with groups or as a whole class on the discussion forum. Alternately, if you used the discussion forum for developing the discussion questions, have them share their experiences live in class.

Again, be sure to be clear with students about what you expect to see in the written discussion. Explicitly ask them to tie the conversations back to class readings or concepts and to cite sources. You'll find that having small but specific requirements will help students to create higher-quality posts.

These five ideas are just the beginning of how you can use a discussion board in a flipped classroom. As you consider activities that will work well in your own courses, remember to be thoughtful in your use of the discussion board and determine why it is the best format for the conversation to occur. Don't just use the discussion board because it is there. In many cases, having face-to-face conversations is more effective. But, as identified in the examples above, a discussion board can be an effective tool to facilitate the flow between the online and face-to-face portions of your class.

Adapted from the Magna 20-Minute Mentor presentation, *Beyond the Discussion Board: How Can I Engage Online Students?*

Flipping the Feedback: "Screencasting" Written Feedback on Student Essays

by Ron Martinez, PhD

L ast semester I was faced with two sections of a senior composition class for English majors, both larger than usual—which of course also meant a larger-than-usual feedback load. With a new baby at home, I was more than a little concerned about time. Fully aware of the research (e.g., Ferris, 1997; Hyland and Hyland 2006) that favors more detailed feedback on student writing (seems "awkward: reword" just doesn't cut it), I could not in good conscience consider reducing the quality or quantity of the feedback I usually give. Moreover, my feedback would typically include holding "writing conferences" (one-on-one consultations) with students—usually during office hours. But this was a large class, and there are only so many hours in a day. I knew something had to give.

Having already tested the limits of the physical word, I turned to the less bounded virtual one for help. I had learned anecdotally of professors who sent voice podcasts of their feedback along with their written feedback, which seemed like a nifty idea. But, I thought, what if students could actually watch and hear me in a video as I go over their paper? If possible (which it is), that would approximate the kind of feedback experience I aimed to offer students.

Screencasting (recording and narrating actions performed by the instructor on a computer screen), I discovered, can indeed be an effective medium for feedback, and in some ways can even be better than offering feedback (especially initial feedback) in person.

Below I describe and comment on how it all unfolded.

Which software did I choose?

After looking around a bit, a settled on using Screencast-O-Matic (the first 15 minutes are free) installed on my PC computer, but I know that Quicktime and other packages can work just as well.

What was the feedback process?

Students would submit their completed take-home writing assignments electronically. Especially for shorter assignments (fewer than three pages), I would only briefly skim over the text, and then launch Screencast-O-Matic to record my feedback in real time. In other words, students would see any highlighting, underlining, or suggested changes happen as I was making them on their Word documents. In effect, students would hear me "dialoguing" with them as I narrated what I was doing, why I was doing it, and what I was thinking throughout the feedback process. I would then return the marked-up document to students via email, along with a link to the (private) YouTube upload. To understand the written feedback, students would need to watch the video. A short example of an early attempt at screencasting feedback can be seen here: youtube.com/watch?v=gSZhNWCwSjA.

What did the students do with the feedback?

I recorded screencasts for all first drafts, and students were then required to redraft. And that's where the flipped part comes in. In most cases students would watch the screencasts before class, sometimes attempting a redraft at home, other times waiting to come to class to ask follow-up questions. On other occasions, particularly with feedback on longer essays, I was unable to get the screencasts back to students until just the night before class (did I mention I have a toddler son at home?), in which case, the students would actually watch their videos at the outset of class on their various devices (kind of like having multiple versions of me talking to the students simultaneously about their papers), followed by in-class redrafting.

After the students had become accustomed to receiving and redrafting using screencast feedback, students were invited to try it out for themselves. This exercise was well-received, with most students opting to give each other screencast feedback, reporting that it allowed them to give much more feedback than they normally would if limited to written feedback only. (Indeed, this was evinced by the duration of the feedback delivered by students, with a few producing feedback lasting over 30 minutes.) Furthermore, as in the case of this particular semester—there were two sections of the same class, one in the morning and one in the evening—I decided to have the morning group read the other section's papers, and vice-versa. Screencasting proved immensely valuable for this exercise.

What were some positive takeaways from the whole exercise?

Unable to meet with students and produce the quantity and quality of feedback I usually aim for, screencasting proved an excellent alternative. Rather than just seeing a static comment, correction code, or other marking on a page, students got a much greater and richer feedback experience. To put it another way, the screencasting medium allowed me to elaborate on why a particular word or phrase seemed "awkward," and how a student might go about rewording it.

However, I also realized that there were even some pluses that made screencasting arguably better than my usual writing conferences. For example, this particular class was comprised entirely of non-native speakers of English, thus potentially reducing the effectiveness of in-person conferences due to oral comprehension issues. However, one nice aspect of the screen-cast feedback is that it could also serve as a record of the feedback—one that students could pause, rewind, replay, and review whenever and as many times as needed.

Another unexpected plus came from the "flipping"—particularly the in-class redrafting. What started as a kind of stop-gap measure because of late-night, last-minute feedback (i.e., students viewing the screencasts to start the class), eventually emerged as a productive activity that made good use of class time, turning the class into individualized writing workshops.

Anything negative?

It would be disingenuous to suggest that screencasting was a timesaver. It wasn't. In some cases the screencasting took about as much time as I would normally expend giving just written feedback; on other occasions—in particular for longer papers—the reading followed by oral commentary involved much more time than one would expect to spend if just writing in the margins of a student's essay. But that was never the point of giving feedback a try in the first place. Feedback through screencasting allowed me to provide a kind of writing conference experience for my students while not tying me (or the feedback) to a particular time or space.

What did the students think?

Midway through the semester I asked students complete a survey midway through the course (responses were anonymous), and all students wrote that they wanted to continue receiving feedback via screencast, and only one (out of 23) said that screencast feedback was not preferable to written feedback alone. Students were also asked to comment on what they liked about screencast feedback, and here are a few representative quotations:

"I really liked the audio feedback because it was complete. Sometimes when I got feedback in other classes I couldn't understand some parts of the corrections, but now with the video I was able to understand what the professor meant."

"I liked hearing and seeing what my problems were, rather than just seeing marks on a page. I like the explanations about what my writing issues are."

"Video feedback was really useful to better understand what the professor means and how I can improve my draft. I hope you keep doing it!"

Recommendations and Advice

- It helps to talk with students about the importance of feedback, and why you have chosen screencasting as an option.
- Although many computers (especially notebook computers) have built-in microphones, I found that the quality of using VOIP-type headphones enhanced the audio quality.
- Develop a feedback coding system that works for you (i.e., color-coded highlighting), which can be created together with your students.
- Read the students' work first before screencasting, using the coding system while reading to mark places you wish to verbally comment on during the screencast.
- Depending on the purpose of the written assignment (and the feedback), you can make corrections and more specific comments that you can simply refer to during the screencast (for example, "There are a number of places where I have suggested vocabulary changes, which you can see for yourself") so that you make the most of the screencast time and the advantages afforded by the medium.
- The first couple of times you screencast feedback, it helps to remind students what the codes mean. (For example, "As a reminder, the parts I have highlighted in green are there to point out things I liked in your paper, and the parts in blue are points that I think should be reformulated.")
- Try delivering your feedback according to the coding system. (For

example, "Let me start with the parts in green.")

- The 15-minute time frame in the free version of the software I used seemed to work well as a limit for my students' papers (which were never longer than 3,000 words). The time limit usefully forced me to focus on the main issues I wanted to students to notice for the re-drafting process.
- Screencasting is also useful for more summative feedback (for example, end-of-semester comments). It allowed me to comment extensively on the students' body of work as whole, and how well they had progressed.
- After students become accustomed to the screencast feedback, experiment with getting students to give each other feedback via screencasting.

Reprinted from *Faculty Focus,* January 8, 2016.

Can You Flip an Online Class? Seven Flipped Strategies to Enhance Engagement

by Barbi Honeycutt, PhD and Sarah Glova

We recently asked a group of teaching assistants, "How do you think today's college classroom is different than when you were an undergraduate student? What is the most significant change you've noticed?"

The number one answer? Technology.

This is not a surprise. What's most interesting is that many of these graduate students were undergraduates just a few years ago, yet they still see technology as the most significant change in the college classroom. Why? Shouldn't our students be used to it by now? Shouldn't we? Either technology is changing so rapidly that we always see it as "new," or we're still struggling to integrate technology effectively and seamlessly into the learning experience. Or maybe it's both.

Many have argued that education seems to be "the last frontier" for technological disruption (Blin and Munro 2008; Christensen, C., Aaron, and Clark 2002; Christensen 2002; Magid 2013). Is it because the culture of higher education is hesitant to change? Are we waiting for research to show how this change influences learning? Are we receiving the support we need to implement technology effectively? Are we concerned about the automatization of education? Do we struggle to use today's technology because most of it wasn't available when we were students? Are we seeing technology as a barrier between the students and us?

The answer to these questions is most likely some degree of "Yes." We know the challenges and benefits of teaching and learning with technology.

But we also know there's something special about the learning experiences we share with our students in the face-to-face classroom. The face-to-face learning experience just can't be replicated, yet many of us keep trying to recreate it with technology.

But maybe that's the wrong approach. Perhaps we shouldn't try to "replicate" those face-to-face learning experiences. Instead, we should try to find the technological tools that allow us to adapt the strategies we use in our face-to-face classes to engage with and connect to our students in the online environment, just in a different way.

One way to address this is to apply the flipped philosophy to the online classroom. The flipped classroom model can help us design more interactive and engaging online learning experiences, and online classes can help us expand on what it means to flip. Certainly there is something to learn by combining these two conversations.

During the past few years, the flipped classroom has been defined as reversing what happens "in" and "out" of the classroom. Some scholars define the flip even more specifically as reversing homework and lectures where students watch videos of lectures for homework "out of class" and then engage in problem-solving and analysis "in class."

But what happens when we apply this flipped model to an online class? The "in" class and "out of class" terminology doesn't work. In the online class, what exactly is "class time" and what is "before class time?" If the definition of the flipped classroom always distinguishes between "in class" and "out of class," how can we apply the flipped approach to an online class? This is why we need to expand the definition of the flip (Honeycutt and Glova 2013).

In our work, we continue to push the conversations toward more comprehensive definitions of the flip. Our philosophy comes from the idea that the FLIP is to Focus on your Learners by Involving them in the Process. At its core, the flip means shifting the focus from the instructor to the students. You can do this by inverting the design of the course so students engage in activities, apply concepts, and focus on higher-level learning outcomes (Honeycutt and Garrett 2013). Using this definition, the flip moves away from being defined as only something that happens in class vs. out of class. Instead, we focus on what students are doing to construct knowledge, connect with others, and engage in higher levels of critical thinking and analysis.

This applies to both the online and face-to-face environment. The real flip is not about where activities take place—it's about flipping the focus from you to your students. In an online class, this could translate to flipping from a "download-and-review" process to an "interact-and-contribute" approach. In download-and-review online classes, students go to an online class space to download resources and assignments or review lecture notes and course materials. In interact-and-contribute online classes, the students' role is flipped; instead of only being the receiver of information, the student goes one step further and is also the supplier of information. The student is interacting with the content and moving or changing it somehow to better understand it. The student then contributes content, submitting edited or original content that helps her (and helps her peers) better understand the course material.

When the focus of the flip is less on what is "before class" and "after class" and more on what the students' role is in the class, then we can flip any environment: in person, online, or hybrid.

Using this expanded definition, what flipped strategies could we integrate into an online class? Here are seven flipped strategies to consider for your online class (or your blended or hybrid class):

1. Create a scavenger hunt.

During the first week of class, create a scavenger hunt with your course website. Ask students to locate important information, announcements, and deadlines. Offer an incentive for the first one to submit the completed scavenger hunt activity. Incentives may include the first choice on presentation topics, the chance to drop a low quiz grade, or the opportunity to gain an extra credit point on the final project. Ask the students to submit their scavenger hunt answers; the submission can become a checklist of important course reminders they can refer back to when they have questions at any time throughout the semester.

Why it works: Students are actively locating information and constructing their own mental models of the course rather than just reading the course web site or listening to a video as you describe the structure and organization of the course.

2. Create a hashtag just for your course.

Encourage students to use this hashtag if they find course-related items in different social media spaces or elsewhere on the web. Make the hashtag unique to your course. Consider reviewing the posts and then sharing an item a week with the entire class. If you're comfortable with social media, you can even create an account and "repost" any content you think everyone should pay attention to, and you could embed that social media feed in your course (so all students—not just those on social media—can see it.)

Why it works: Students are actively contributing to the conversation by sharing resources and information they find rather than just reviewing the content you have collected. They are helping collect and curate content. You can enhance this strategy by encouraging students to go a step further and analyze or evaluate it.

3. Develop a low stakes assignment to encourage self-reflection and analysis.

Ask students to reflect on their own learning styles, preferences, or personalities in the online environment before beginning the semester. Encouraging students to think about this actively might help them to prepare for the online environment as they analyze their strengths, weaknesses, challenges, etc. Supplement this activity by making it a private forum requirement and then post a global response to students afterward with suggestions on how to succeed in the online environment.

Why it works: Students are asked to analyze and evaluate their strengths and weaknesses in regards to a course, activity, or assignment. This can help build their capacity to advance towards higher levels of critical thinking. It also helps to shift their focus; this course is not focused on the instructor delivering content; it is about their responsibility to learn the content. This strategy can help students transition to their role as active participants in the learning environment.

4. Ask the students to teach.

Assign mini-lessons across the semester to individual students or small groups. Be specific about the content they are responsible for such as: what information, what level of detail, and how long the lesson should be. But, be flexible and open about the delivery. Encourage students to go beyond a presentation or lecture. Give them access to a variety of tools and strategies. For example, students might choose to create dynamic PowerPoint decks, narrated Prezi presentations, webinars, or podcasts. Let them choose what works best for their purpose and topic. However, it's important to note that some students might be overwhelmed if there are too many choices. You could narrow their choices by offering only three media options to choose from, for example. The important part of this process is not the technological tool. It's the process of learning how to teach, how to create content, and how to engage others.

Why it works: Learning to teach is a complicated process because it takes more than just knowing the content. With this strategy, students have to learn the content but then they also have to consider the best ways to communicate that information and to encourage their peers to take action. Students feel they are contributing to the online course and making it a shared learning space. This helps them understand that an online course can be more than a space for the instructor to deliver information. And as a bonus, your course will benefit from their varied perspectives and examples.

5. Encourage peer review.

In a traditional class, peer review can be as simple as asking students to bring multiple copies of a working draft. In online spaces, peer review can sometimes feel too cumbersome to tackle. But technology tools are always changing, and they can make online peer review easier than ever. For example, ask students to post their working drafts onto a tool like Google Drive. Then they can share drafts with other students just by sharing a link, and their peers can review their content by making comments directly in the online document. You can also use online forums to create groups where students can post documents and then read the replies of their peers. If you want the reviews to be live, then consider creating synchronous chat spaces—students can email their drafts out ahead of time and then sign into the chat space at the same time, taking turns offering comments to one another and responding to feedback.

Why it works: Peer review is active, engaging, and helpful—it allows students to see each other's work, to benefit from varied perspectives, and to learn how to critique and offer constructive feedback. Also, in an online course, the interaction benefit of peer review is even more paramount; the peer commentary becomes a way to connect, challenge, and recognize fellow students and their work.

6. Draft a whole-class policy, response, or recommendation.

Even if the content of your course isn't particularly political, it could still be appropriate for a public service announcement, public policy statement, or press release. Challenge the students in your class to submit a statement that reflects the lessons learned from the course. This could be a recommendation to government or policy shapers, a helpful reference guide or public service announcement for the general population, or a statement of support or disapproval about a recent event or incident. Ask students to work together using a collaborative space like a Wiki, or ask students to write individual submissions and post all the submissions into the space. Then ask students to find themes and construct a response using the contributions and ideas from their colleagues. Use tools like Wordle to create word clouds, or create an online poll to allow students to vote on the most important statements. Finally, help students identify the intended audience and locate an appropriate place to share their message.

Why it works: Not only does this connect the content of the course to some greater movement, audience, or theme, but it also shares the voices of the students. Whether done as a whole class, in groups, or at the individual level, the challenge of interpreting the lessons of a course for the general public is one that requires higher-level thinking and student engagement.

7. Open your video lecture content to comments.

If you use video lectures as part of your flipped classroom, the online format allows for you to collect more feedback. If you have a small class, this could mean that each video lecture has a space where students can share comments and questions, and theoretically you and other students could post replies to help answer questions. You may decide to participate in these comment areas or not.

Why it works: In a face-to-face class, students have the opportunity to raise their hands to ask questions or react to your lecture. This strategy is the online equivalent to this interaction. You can ask for comments by inviting students through the media itself (for example, "Pause this video now and leave a comment in the chat space, sharing a story of any challenges or breakthroughs you had when first applying this principle"), or you can use the webpage to post instructions about how students can (and why or when students should) comment. Not only will you increase engagement, but you'll also receive something that many online instructors say they wish they had more of—feedback from students.

Conclusion

Flipped strategies shift the focus from the instructor to the students; they encourage active participation rather than passive observation; and, they engage students by encouraging evaluation rather than knowledge recall. Whether a course is entirely face-to-face, entirely online, or blended, you can create student-centered learning experiences in your online environments by finding flippable moments in the digital space. Along the way, you may discover ways that technology can encourage engagement and learning in ways the face-to-face classroom can't.

Reprinted from *Faculty Focus*, March 31, 2014.

CHAPTER 5 REFLECTION AND DISCUSSION QUESTIONS

Use these questions for reflection, discussion, and application as you consider how to organize and plan successful flipped classroom learning experiences.

Reflection and Discussion:
1. What are the advantages and disadvantages to using technological tools such as laptops, tablets, and cell phones during class time?
2. What are the pros and cons to using a feedback approach such as screencasting to give feedback to your students? How would you need to adapt this strategy to work in your classes?
3. Have you taken an online course or training session? What types of activities and tools did the instructor use? What was most helpful for you as a learner in the online space? How can you adapt some of these strategies and tools to use in your online course?

Application:
1. Review the flipped lesson you've been developing throughout this book. Now go back through each of the learning outcomes and activities and brainstorm what types of technological tools will help you and your students be successful. What do you need the tools to do for you? How will these tools help students achieve the learning outcomes?
2. Where do each of the tools best fit into the flipped lesson? Before class, during class, or after class (or all three)? Map each tool to the learning activities so you can begin to get a clear vision of how the tools will support the students' learning process.
3. Take time to research one technological tool or resource you've never used before. Since technology is always changing so rapidly, just try something new and imagine all the possible ways you could use the tool in your classroom. You don't have to build this new tool into this specific lesson. Just go try something new and consider ways you could use it in the future.

Conclusions and Future Directions

Throughout this book, you've explored what the flipped classroom is, why it matters, and how to implement it. It's a good start. But, what's next? After exploring the literature and talking with faculty around the country, here are three ideas for future conversations and research to advance our thinking about flipped learning in higher education (in no particular order):

Increase scholarship

As more faculty experiment with the flipped model, they are starting to conduct scholarship, publish findings, and share their experiences. All of these results are helping us determine what works, what doesn't, and what direction we need to go. In the Flipped Classroom Trends reader survey, more than 70 percent of the respondents indicated it was a positive experience for them as the instructor in the flipped class (2015). And, almost 70 percent of the respondents indicated it was a positive experience for their students (2015). Respondents indicated they saw increased positive gains in student engagement and student learning. These are the types of findings we need to analyze and dig deeper into so we can share the "best practices" with other educators who are interested in implementing the flipped model.

Alternatively, we need to analyze what's happening with the 30 percent who are *not* finding success with the flipped model. What factors contributed to these faculty members feeling like it didn't work? How was "success" defined and measured? Was it the first time the instructor implemented the flip? How much, if any, professional development or training was provided as part of the instructor's decision to flip? Are there prerequisite experiences students need to receive prior to being a student in a flipped classroom? How are we preparing students for their new roles and responsibilities?

And finally, we also need to continue studying the adaptations of the flipped classroom in introductory courses, large classes, online environments, seminar and graduate courses, mobile learning environments and across a wider variety of disciplines. Some work has been done in these areas, but we need more faculty to share their findings so we can continue to advance our thinking and consider what type of environments are (and are not) appropriate for the flipped model. As an interesting side note, in the *Faculty Focus* Flipped Classroom Trends reader survey, some respondents said this model "only works in the humanities," and some respondents said this model "only works in the sciences" (2015). Clearly, we need to share our results beyond the scope of our disciplines.

Update peer review of teaching, recognition, and reward processes

I have visited campuses where the flipped model was a mandate from a senior academic leader, and I have visited campuses where the flipped classroom conversation was part of a grassroots effort by a few motivated faculty. As you can imagine, there are pros and cons to each of these perspectives. In the Flipped Classroom Trends reader survey (2015), I was surprised (and happy) to see how many respondents felt supported by their department heads and deans. This is not the case everywhere I visit. I mention this because it has a significant impact on one of the future directions we need to consider as we advance our conversations about the flipped model in higher education.

We must have more conversations about how faculty are recognized for their efforts to move toward innovative pedagogies such as the flipped classroom. This is a hard one, I know. But it is important. Look at the current peer review of teaching processes on your campus. Do they work with the flipped model? How has the flipped model been defined for the peer reviewer? Has the peer reviewer been "trained" in how the flipped classroom works? What is being measured? Is it student learning? Instructor engagement? Student engagement? And what does "engagement" look like? How do we know a successful flipped learning experience when we see one?

All of these questions lead to larger conversations about how promotion, tenure, and faculty recognition programs are designed. Do we need to adjust some of our processes to reflect the changing role of the instructor in the flipped classroom? What would that look like? How would it work? These are the types of questions that will start to emerge as more faculty integrate the flip into their courses.

Assess and value "transferable skills"

Most of the conversations and scholarship around whether or not the flipped classroom model "works" focus on the measurement of student learning in terms of course content. Quiz scores, exam grades, and discussions about whether or not students can demonstrate mastery of learning outcomes have been the primary measures of "success" of the flipped classroom model. However, we're missing another important outcome of the flip.

What else are students learning in these classrooms beyond the content? How to communicate effectively? How to work in teams? How to lead? How to follow? How to become more self-directed? How to ask better questions? How to create something new? How to handle conflict? These are what I'll call "transferable skills" (since I cringe when I hear the words "soft skills"). Do these types of transferable skills get assessed? Should they? If so, how? Or, are these skills just part of the expected learning experience and aren't part of the assessment and evaluation process? Whether or not you choose to formally assess these skills in your flipped courses, they are an important part of the flipped learning experience.

One of the main challenges of the flipped classroom model is student motivation. How do we get students to come to class prepared? How do we get them to see the value of this type of learning environment? How do we help them work through their resistance to student-centered learning? Maybe part of the answer to these questions lies in these transferable skills. These are skills students would not otherwise gain if they didn't have the opportunity to learn in a flipped environment. As we conduct more scholarship on the flipped model, let's start looking beyond test scores and exams to measure success.

Final thoughts

These are just a few possible directions to move our conversations about the flipped classroom forward. In a few years—if it's not happening already—more of your students will come to your classroom having already been a learner in flipped learning environments. Depending on their prior experiences, they may bring negative baggage into your classroom solely based on their association with the flipped classroom model. This may create more resistance. Or, alternatively, you may have *more* students demanding active, student-centered learning experiences where they do something together because they understand the purpose. They know the challenges but they see the value. We can hope anyway.

It's been an interesting journey to watch the flipped classroom conversation unfold. As I bring this book to a close, I hope you have been inspired to try something new and create successful flipped learning experiences for yourself and your students. I also hope this book sets the stage for advancing our conversations about the flipped model in higher education.

Now, let's go "flip it!"

APPENDIX

Flipped Classroom Trends—A Survey of College Faculty

Perhaps no other word has been as popular in higher education during the past few years as the term "flipped." As a result, there is no shortage of ideas and opinions about flipped learning environments. Some consider it another way to talk about student-centered learning. Others view flipped classrooms as an entirely new approach to teaching and learning. Still others see flipping as just another instructional fad that will eventually run its course.

In the summer of 2014, *Faculty Focus* surveyed its readers to gain a better understanding of their views on flipped learning. The survey also sought to find out who's flipping, who's not, and the barriers and benefits to those who flip.

Defining the flipped classroom

One of the most interesting themes that emerged from this survey is the amount of confusion about what "flipped" means. Much of the contention about whether a flipped classroom leads to enhanced learning seems to point toward the different ways educators define or conceptualize it.

When asked to define/describe the flipped classroom in their own words, respondents varied in their description. Some relied on the definitions related to leveraging technology (i.e., videos of lectures), while others described it in terms of active, student-centered, collaborative learning strategies.

The terminology and definitions are causing confusion, but most scholars and survey respondents seem to agree that active learning and student-centered learning approaches are the foundational principles of the flipped philosophy, and the value of this approach is that it can lead to enhanced student engagement, motivation, and learning, if done well.

Key findings

Results from the survey are based on the responses from the 1,089 *Faculty Focus* readers who completed the survey. Highlights include:

- More than two-thirds (69.5 percent) have tried flipping an activity, class, period, or course, and plan to do it again. Another 5.49 percent have tried flipping, but don't plan to do it again.

- Roughly one-third (31.8 percent) of those who have flipped did so within the past year.
- The majority of faculty who have flipped rated the experience as positive for themselves (70.3 percent) and their students (64.8 percent).
- The top reasons for flipping include a desire to increase student engagement (79.3 percent) and improve student learning (75.8 percent).
- In terms of the actual benefits, nearly three-fourths did see greater student engagement (74.9 percent), while just over half saw evidence of improved student learning (54.6 percent).
- More than 80 percent said students are more collaborative and 76.6 percent said they ask more questions, while almost half (48.7 percent) also noted some student resistance.
- The most frequently reported barrier for faculty who want to try flipping is limited time. Nearly 70 percent said it was a very significant challenge (38 percent) or a significant challenge (31.6 percent).
- Of those respondents who are not interested in flipped learning, 38.9 percent said they don't know enough about it and 27.4 percent felt it was a fad.

Methods

This survey was conducted between June 15, 2014, and July 20, 2014. An email was sent to 128,611 *Faculty Focus* subscribers inviting them to participate in the survey. The mailing list consisted largely of faculty at all levels, but also included administrators, instructional designers, and faculty developers. Respondents represented higher education institutions from the United States and Canada, as well as a small number of institutions abroad.

The survey was anonymous, using the SurveyMonkey web tool. It featured 18 questions total, including both qualitative and quantitative formats (multiple choice and open-ended questions). A total of 1,089 people completed it. Respondents were asked:

INDICATE THE EXTENT TO WHICH YOU AGREE OR DISAGREE WITH THE FOLLOWING STATEMENTS RELATED TO STUDENTS IN YOUR FLIPPED COURSE:

They are more engaged

Respondents overwhelmingly found students in flipped classrooms to be more engaged than students in traditional classrooms. More than half (51.6 percent) of respondents agreed strongly with the statement, and another 38.5 percent agreed somewhat. Less than 10 percent of respondents disagreed at all, with 5.6 percent disagreeing somewhat and 4.2 percent disagreeing strongly.

Their grades are improving

The majority of respondents saw a positive correlation between the flipped classroom and student grades. More than 58 percent agreed somewhat and 19 percent agreed strongly that grades improved for students in flipped classrooms.

However, there was some dissent among the survey participants. Nearly a quarter of respondents did not see a relationship between flipping and better grades. Of this group, 17.3 percent disagreed somewhat with the statement, and another 5.2 percent disagreed strongly.

They are resistant

Survey participants were split almost evenly on whether students are resistant to flipping. Nearly half indicated that they either somewhat agreed (38.1 percent) or strongly agreed (10.6 percent) with the statement. Slightly more than half disagreed, with 34.9 percent of respondents disagreeing somewhat and 16.2 percent disagreeing strongly.

They adapt to the approach

Again, with 85 percent agreeing with the statement, respondents overwhelmingly believed that students could adapt to a flipped classroom. Nearly 30 percent strongly agreed that students adapt to flipping, while 55.4 percent agreed somewhat. Less than 15 percent disagreed at all, with 11.9 percent disagreeing somewhat and only 2.7 percent disagreeing strongly.

They ask more questions

Respondents also believed students asked more questions in a flipped classroom than in a traditional classroom. Approximately 40 percent somewhat agreed with the statement, while 37.1 percent agreed strongly that students asked more questions in a flipped learning environment. Less than a quarter of survey participants disagreed, with 19.3 percent disagreeing somewhat and 4.1 percent disagreeing strongly.

They come to class more prepared

Many survey participants also found that students arrived better prepared for a flipped class. Nearly a quarter strongly agreed with the statement, while 42.9 percent agreed somewhat. However, the responses were not entirely positive, reflecting some of the flipping criticisms (e.g. that some students will not prepare regardless of the motivations built into the course) present throughout the comments to the survey. Nearly a quarter (23.9 percent) disagreed somewhat, and 8.5 percent strongly disagreed that students are better prepared in a flipped classroom.

They are more collaborative

The vast majority (more than 80 percent) of respondents believed that flipping encourages students to be more collaborative. More than 39 percent strongly agreed and 43.9 percent agreed somewhat with the statement. Only 13.1 percent disagreed somewhat, and even fewer (3.8 percent) disagreed strongly. These answers reflect the actual practice of flipped instruction, which almost always involves regular group work during class time. Students have more opportunity to collaborate in a flipped classroom, and the frequent practice could improve their collaboration skills.

They see the value of this type of experience

Nearly three-quarters of survey participants felt that students are aware of the value of a flipped classroom. More than half (50.07 percent) agreed somewhat and 23.1 percent agreed strongly. However, there was some disagreement. Slightly fewer than 21 percent disagreed somewhat that students recognize the value of a flipped classroom, while 6 percent disagreed strongly.

They are comfortable using the technology

Respondents largely do not perceive technology to be a concern for students in a flipped classroom. More than half agreed somewhat and 32.2 percent agreed strongly that students are comfortable with the technology used in flipped classrooms. Less than 20 percent disagreed at all, with 12.6 percent disagreeing somewhat and only 4.7 percent disagreeing strongly. Some comments to other questions in this survey reflect the concern that flipping presumes students will have access to computers and tablets outside of class, and students are disadvantaged in the flipped classroom when they don't.

They build relationships/community

Again, survey respondents identified another benefit of the flipped classroom. Nearly 80 percent indicated that students build relationships and community when in a flipped learning environment, with 48.4 percent agreeing somewhat and 31.4 percent agreeing strongly. Around 20 percent did not find that to be true, with 15.25 percent disagreeing somewhat and 4.99 percent disagreeing strongly.

Indicate the extent to which you agree or disagree with each of the following statements related to students in your flipped course(s): (Total: 761)

	Agree strongly	Agree somewhat	Disagree somewhat	Disagree strongly
They are more engaged	51.64%	38.50%	5.65%	4.20%
Their grades are improving	19.05%	58.34%	17.35%	5.26%
They are resistant	10.64%	38.11%	34.95%	16.29%
They adapt to the approach	29.83%	55.45%	11.96%	2.76%
They ask more questions	37.19%	39.42%	19.32%	4.07%
They come to class prepared	24.57%	42.97%	23.92%	8.54%
They are more collaborative	39.16%	43.89%	13.14%	3.81%
They see the value of this type of experience	23.13%	50.07%	20.76%	6.04%
They are comfortable using the technology	32.19%	50.46%	12.61%	4.73%
They build relationships/ community	31.41%	48.36%	15.24%	4.99%

What were the biggest benefits experienced from flipping?

The survey offered participants 10 different choices and the option to select multiple answers. Most of the respondents indicated that flipping positively influenced student learning and the classroom-learning environment. More specifically, nearly three-quarters (74.9 percent) of respondents indicated that their students were more engaged when learning in a flipped environment. Two-thirds (66.6 percent) felt that flipping created a more learner-centered class environment, and just over half (54.7 percent) believed that the method improved student learning as well. Half of respondents indicated that flipping improved the learning environment. These actual benefits of flipping align closely with the reasons instructors wanted to try flipping, as indicated in the previous question (Why did you decide to start flipping?).

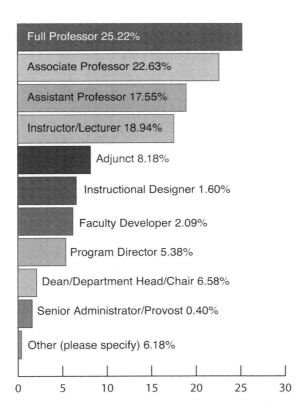

Survey answers revealed that respondents personally benefited from flipping, too. Many instructors (41.26 percent) indicated that through flipping they were able to get to know their students better. Nearly just as many (39.8 percent) reported that flipping made them more excited to teach. Almost a third (31.1 percent) of participants indicated that they looked forward to class more often when they incorporated flipping into their pedagogy, and nearly as many (30.35 percent) said that flipping re-energized their courses.

Many respondents (27.99 percent) indicated that their colleagues not only took notice of their flipping but also asked respondents to share their methodology. Another 14.3 percent were able to produce scholarship about the approach and their experiences.

Some survey participants who tried flipping identified advantages they did not expect. One respondent from a public, four-year university indicated that he could cover more material when he used a flipped approach. Another full professor in visual and performing arts from a private, four-year institution said that the process of preparing lectures for preclass consumption actually improved the delivery of live lectures (e.g., phrasing and posture) as well. Still another lecturer from a public, four-year institution noted that flipping was particularly beneficial to individuals with learning disabilities or who were not native English speakers. "Dyslexic [students] and students with English as a second language," he said, "closed the performance gap by, on average, a whole grade boundary."

However, not all unanticipated outcomes were beneficial. When given the opportunity to elaborate, some respondents indicated that flipping is a great approach for students who are already motivated but less so for the others. Others responded that they did not anticipate the amount of preparation that flipping would require. According to an associate professor at a private, four-year institution, flipping "requires much more work on the front end than simply preparing and delivering a lecture."

Another instructor from a public, four-year institution agreed. "There is more work involved," the respondent wrote. "It takes more preparation and more emotional energy to be this involved with students."

What challenges do you face when you think about flipping your class?

Many barriers exist for faculty who want to experiment with innovative teaching approaches. The move to a flipped classroom isn't an easy transition for many faculty. They may not be supported by their department head, dean, or academic leader. They may not be rewarded or recognized for taking time to develop innovative approaches to teaching. They may not receive funding/support to embark on a full-course redesign.

In an effort to identify the biggest barriers to flipping, this question asked participants to indicate which challenges exist and to rate how significant those challenges are.

Respondents identified several limiting factors, the greatest of which was time. More than 38 percent of survey participants indicated that time was very significant and always a challenge. Another 31.6 percent said time was significant and often a challenge. That is nearly 70 percent of all respondents who see time as a frequent, if not constant, barrier to flipping. Another 19.4 percent of respondents said time was sometimes a factor, rating it a moderate challenge, while just over 10 percent said it was never a challenge. This echoes earlier open-ended responses, in which instructors who tried flipping indicated that it was more time-consuming than they had anticipated (and than traditional lecturing).

Respondents indicated that other professional responsibilities required by their positions were the next most common barrier. Just over half said that this was a significant (29.2 percent) or very significant (21.7 percent) challenge, while another 28.2 percent said it was a moderate challenge. About one of every five respondents (20.9 percent) said competing responsibilities were insignificant barriers or rarely a challenge.

Respondents also identified that the idea of flipping made them feel pressure to be creative and develop new strategies and ideas. Nearly 45 percent of all respondents indicated that these tactical concerns about implementing the activity- based approach challenged them significantly (29.85 percent) or very significantly (14.98 percent). About another third (33.3 percent) believed the need to be creative and introduce new strategies would be a moderate challenge for them.

Survey participants conveyed a fear that students might resist the approach or lack the motivation to do the pre-class work that would first expose them to course content. While more respondents show greater concern regarding time and conflicting priorities, concerns about student resistance and lack of motivation were also significant. More than 80 percent of respondents indicated that they worried about student objections or ambivalence when they considered flipping instruction. Even so, it doesn't appear that the group of respondents found these challenges to be insurmountable. The largest group (37.8 percent) considered these challenges to be moderate, while just over a quarter found them significant (26.4 percent) and fewer still (18 percent) found them to be very significant.

Other issues, such as lack of institutional support evidenced by insufficient resources, funding, or space, were concerns for more than two-thirds of survey participants, although much of this group (30.4 percent of all respondents) characterized those insufficiencies as moderate challenges. Only 16.3 percent identified a lack of institutional support as a very significant challenge, and 22.3 percent considered it a significant challenge.

More than half of the respondents revealed some apprehension regarding technology, with 37.1 percent of survey participants considering it a moderate challenge. Another 16.9 percent found their experience or comfort level with technology to be a significant challenge, and yet only 4.2 percent considered it to be a very significant challenge. This response echoed some of the open-ended comments from earlier questions in the survey. While flipping does not require the use of new technology, teaching in higher education today means it can and often does. Some instructors who flip incorporate prerecorded lectures and other audio and visual tools during in-class assignments. For educators with limited exposure to new technologies, this can seem daunting. Also, adjunct instructors, who lack awareness of or access to campus educational technology resources, might feel pressure to invest in technologies or training on their own time and with their own resources.

Respondents indicated that they were less concerned about colleagues or administrators misunderstanding or undervaluing the practice. Nearly half (47.25 percent) indicated that "not being valued" was rarely a challenge, while 41.6 percent reported that being misunderstood was almost never a problem, either. These issues were sometimes challenges that survey respondents faced, but only 16.7 percent (value) and 19.16 percent (understanding) found them to be significant. Fewer still (8.1 percent and 10.1 percent) said that undervaluing or misunderstanding flipping was a very significant concern that always created challenges.

Less than half of respondents found competing goals a problem, with more than half of those (or 26.98 percent of total survey participants) characterizing that conflict as only a moderate challenge.

What type of courses have you flipped or plan to flip?

About two-thirds of respondents had flipped or planned to flip an undergraduate course. Introductory courses were popular (44.2 percent), but survey participants indicated that a broad range of courses had been or would be flipped. These included graduate courses (21.2 percent), capstones and other senior-level courses (16.5percent), professional development (16.7 percent, which included training and continuing education), labs (14.9 percent), and online education (14.4 percent).

Open-ended responses indicated that educators were considering flipping in medical and law school, hybrid courses, and developmental courses.

**What challenges do you face when thinking about flipping your class?
(Total: 908)**

	Very significant/ always a challenge	Significant/ often a challenge	Moderate/ sometimes a challenge	Insignifcant/ rarely a challenge
Time	38.11%	31.61%	19.38%	10.90%
Lack of support (funding/space)	16.30%	22.36%	30.40%	30.95%
Competing department/ college/campus goals	7.93%	14.76%	26.98%	50.33%
Not valued by colleagues/ administration	8.15%	16.74%	27.86%	47.25%
Not understood by colleagues/ administration	10.13%	19.16%	29.07%	41.63%
Being creative/ developing new strategies and ideas	14.98%	29.85%	33.26%	21.92%
Student resistance/lack of motivation	18.06%	26.43%	37.78%	17.73%
My experience/ comfort with technology	4.19%	16.96%	37.11%	41.74%
Other responsibilities required by my position	21.70%	29.19%	28.19%	20.93%

Nearly half of respondents (45.48 percent) either had flipped or planned to flip a class with fewer than 25 students. The next largest group

(32.1 percent) had used or would use flipping in classes with 26 to 50 students. Only around 20 percent would consider or had tried flipping in larger classrooms, with 7.49 percent finding it appropriate for 51 to 75 students and 4.85 percent feeling the same about 76 to 100 students. Even though instructors seemed to favor flipping for smaller groups of students, 8.5 percent of respondents saw a use for flipping in large classes with more than 100 students.

References

Angelo, T. A. and K.P. Cross. 1993. *Classroom assessment techniques: A handbook for college teachers.* San Francisco: Jossey-Bass.

Barkley, E. F., C.H. Major, and K.P. Cross. 2014). *Collaborative learning techniques: A resource for college faculty.* 2nd edition. San Francisco: Jossey-Bass.

Belanoff, P. 1991. The myths of assessment. *Journal of Basic Writing* 10 (1): 54–66.

Bergmann, J. and A. Sams. 2012. *Flip your classroom: Reach every student in every class every day.* Eugene, OR: International Society for Technology in Education.

Blin, F. and M. Munro. 2008. Why hasn't technology disrupted academics' teaching practices? Understanding resistance to change through the lens of activity theory. *Computers and Education* 50 (2): 475–490.

Bonwell, C. and T. Sutherland. 1996. The active learning continuum: Choosing activities to engage students in the classroom. *New Directions for Teaching and Learning* 67 (Fall): 3–16.

Bransford, J. D., Ann L. Brown, and Rodney R. Cocking, eds. 2002. *How people learn: Brain, mind, experience, and school.* Washington, DC: National Academy Press.

Cain, S. 2012. *The power of introverts in a world that can't stop talking.* New York: Crown.

Caswell, N. 2014. Dynamic patterns: Emotional episodes within teachers' response practices. *Journal of Writing Assessment* 7 (1).

Center for Applied Special Technology. 2011. UDL guidelines–educator worksheet. *CAST UDL Online Modules.* http://udlonline.cast.org/guidelines

Center for Applied Special Technology. 2013. *About UDL.* http://cast.org/udl/index.html.

Center for Applied Special Technology. 2014. *UDL on campus: Universal Design for Learning in higher education—A guide.* http://udloncampus.cast.org/

Chen, B., et al. 2015. Students' mobile learning practices in higher education: A multi-year study. *EDUCAUSE Review.* http://er.educause.edu/articles/2015/6/students-mobile-learning-practices-in-higher-education-a-multiyear-study.

Chesborough, S. 1999. Do social work students learn differently? MBTI implications for teaching that address social work students' current learning styles. *Journal of Psychological Type* 69 (2): 23–41. Center for Psychological Type, Inc.

Christensen, C. Improving higher education through disruption. *Forum Futures,* 2002. http://www.educause.edu/ir/library/pdf/ffp0201s.pdf

Christensen, C., S. Aaron, and W. Clark. 2002. Disruption in education. In M. Devlin, R. Larson, and J. Meyerson, eds. The internet and the university. *Forum,* 2001. https://www.educause.edu/ir/library/pdf/ffpiu013.pdf

Cohen, E. G. 1994. Restructuring the classroom: Conditions for productive small groups. *Review of Educational Research* 64 (1): 1–35.

Davidson, M. 2006. Universal design: The work of disability in an age of globalization. *The Disability Studies Reader,* ed. Lennard Davis, 117–130. New York: Routledge.

Davidson, N. and C. Major. 2014. "Crossing boundaries: Collaborative learning, cooperative learning, and problem-based learning." *Journal on Excellence in College Teaching* 25 (3–4): 7–56.

Drinkwater, M. J. et al. 2014. Managing active learning processes in large first-year physics classes: The advantages of an integrated approach. *Teaching and Learning Inquiry: The ISSOTL Journal* 2 (2), 75-90.

EDUCAUSE. 2012. *7 things you should know about flipped classrooms.*
https://net.educause.edu/ir/library/pdf/eli7081.pdf

Ehlers, T. 2014. Online education is the future of learning. *Method Test Prep* blog. http://info.methodtestprep.com/blog/online-education-is-the-future-of-learning.

Faculty Focus. 2015. Flipped classroom trends: A survey of college faculty. Madison, WI: Magna Publications. http://www.facultyfocus.com/free-reports/flipped-classroom-trends-a-survey-of-college-faculty/

Felder, R. and L. Silverman 1988. Learning and teaching styles in engineering education. *Engineering Education* 78 (7): 674–681.

Ferris, D. 1997. The influence of teacher commentary on student revision. *TESOL Quarterly* 31 (2): 315–339.

Flipped Learning Network (FLN). 2014. The Four Pillars of F-L-I-P™

http://flippedlearning.org/wp-content/uploads/2016/07/FLIP_handout_FNL_Web.pdf

Fried, C. B. 2006. In-class laptop use and its effects on student learning. *Computers & Education* 50: 906–914.

Fulton, K. 2012. Upside down and inside out: Flip your classroom to improve student learning. *Learning & Leading with Technology.* ISTE (International Society for Technology in Education).

Gredler, M. E. and C.C. Shields. 2008. *Vygotsky's legacy: A foundation for research and practice.* New York: Guilford Press.

Hembrooke, H. and G. Gay. 2003. The laptop and thel ecture: The effects of multitasking in learning environments. *Journal of Computing in Higher Education* 15 (1).

Honeycutt, B. 2012. *101 ways to FLIP!* FLIP It Consulting. Raleigh, NC.

Honeycutt, B. 2013. Looking for "flippable moments" in your class. *Faculty Focus*. http://www.facultyfocus.com/articles/instructional-design/looking-for-flippable-moments-in-your-cla**ss/**

Honeycutt, B. 2016a. *Ten ways to encourage students to complete the pre-class work in flipped and active learning classrooms.* FLIP It Consulting. Raleigh, NC.

Honeycutt, B. 2016b. *FLIP the first five minutes of class: 50 focusing activities to engage your students.* FLIP It Consulting. Raleigh, NC.

Honeycutt, B. 2016. *Three ways you can use index cards to FLIP your class: Another 'unplugged' flipped strategy.* FLIP It Consulting. Raleigh, NC. http://www.flipitconsulting.com/3-ways-to-use-index-cards-to-flip-your-class/

Honeycutt, B. and J. Garrett, J. 2013. *The flipped approach to a learner-centered class.* Madison, WI: Magna Publications.

Honeycutt, B. and S. Glova. 2013. *101 Ways to FLIP an Online Class.* FLIP It Consulting. Raleigh, NC.

Hyland, K., and F. Hyland. 2006. "Interpersonal aspects of response: Constructing and interpreting teacher written feedback" In *Feedback in second language writing: Contexts and issues.* Cambridge: Cambridge University Press.

Jung, C. G. 1971. *Psychological Types.* Princeton, NJ: Princeton University Press.

Major, C.H., M. Harris, and T. Zakrajsek. 2015. *101 intentionally designed educational activities to put students on the path to success.* London: Routledge.

Lage, M., G. Platt, and M. Treglia. 2000. Inverting the classroom: A gateway to creating an inclusive learning environment. *Journal of Economic Education* 31 (1): 30–43.

Livingston, D. 2006. "Differentiated instruction and assessment in the college classroom." Paper presented at the 12th Annual Conference on College and University Teaching. Kennesaw, Georgia.

Lorenzetti, J. P. 2013. How to create assessments for the flipped classroom. *Faculty Focus*. Madison, WI: Magna Publications.

Magid, L. 2013. "Can technology disrupt education?" *Forbes*, February 26. http://www.forbes.com/sites/larrymagid/2013/02/26/can-technology-disrupt-education/

Matthews, R.S. 1996. "Collaborative learning: Creating knowledge with students." In *Teaching on Solid Ground*, by Robert J. Menges and Maryellen Weimer. San Francisco: Jossey-Bass.

Monahan, N. October 28, 2013. Keeping introverts in mind in your active learning class. *Faculty Focus*. Madison, WI: Magna Publications. http://www.facultyfocus.com/articles/teaching-and-learning/keeping-introverts-in-mind-in-your-active-learning-classroom/

Plotnikoff, D. 2013. "Classes should do hands-on exercises before reading and video, Stanford researchers say." *Stanford Report*. http://news.stanford.edu/news/2013/july/flipped-learning-model-071613.html.

Rose, D., et al. 2006. Universal design for learning in postsecondary education: Reflections on principles and their application. *Journal of Postsecondary Education and Disability* 19 (2): 17. http://www.udlcenter.org/sites/udlcenter.org/files/UDLinPostsecondary.pdf.

Sams, A. and B. Bennett. 2012. "The truth about flipped learning." *eSchool News*. http://www.eschoolnews.com/2012/05/31/the-truth-about-flipped-learning/

Sana, F., T. Weston, and N. Cepeda. 2013. Laptop multitasking hinders classroom learning for both users and nearby peers. *Computers & Education* 62: 24–31.

Silverthorn, D. U. 2006. Teaching and learning in the interactive classroom. *Advances in Physiology Education* 30:135–140.

Stiggins, R. J., et al. 2004. *Classroom assessment for student learning: Doing it right—Using it well.* Portland, OR: Assessment Training Institute.

Stodden, R. A., S. Brown, and K. Roberts. 2011. Disability-friendly university environments: Conducting a climate assessment. *New Directions for Higher Education* 1 (154): 83–92.

Strayer, J. F. 2012. How learning in an inverted classroom influences cooperation, innovation and task orientation. *Learning Environments Research* 15 (2): 171–193.

Sweet, M. and L.K. Michaelsen. 2012. *Critical thinking and engagement: Team-based learning in the social sciences and humanities.* Sterling, VA: Stylus Publishing.

Talbert, R. March 4, 2014. The inverted calculus course: Using guided practice to build self-regulation. Casting Out Nines series. *Chronicle of Higher Education.* http://bit.ly/1kWlBoT

Talbert, R. April 1, 2014. Toward a common definition of flipped learning. Casting Out Nines series. *The Chronicle of Higher Education.* http://chronicle.com/blognetwork/castingoutnines/2014/04/01/toward-a-common-definition-of-flipped-learning/

Wiggins, G. P., and J. McTighe. 2005. *Understanding by design.* Alexandria, VA: Association for Supervision and Curriculum Development.

Weimer, M. 2014. Does it matter what we call it? *The Teaching Professor* 28 (3): 4.

Yancey, K. 1998. *Reflection in the writing classroom.* Logan, UT: Utah State University Press.

About the Editor

Barbi Honeycutt, PhD, is a speaker, scholar, and author. Throughout the past 16 years, she has facilitated more than 3,000 professional development events for more than 15,000 faculty, graduate students, and postdocs around the world.

Dr. Honeycutt is the founder of FLIP It Consulting in Raleigh, NC, and an adjunct professor. The "FLIP" means to "Focus on your Learners by Involving them in the Process."

Prior to launching her own educational consulting business full time, she was the director of graduate student teaching programs and the director of the faculty center for teaching and learning at North Carolina State University. Dr. Honeycutt has published several articles and books based on her FLIP framework, teaching and learning in higher education, faculty development, and graduate student professional development.

About the Contributors

Howard E. Aldrich is a Kenan professor of sociology; adjunct professor of business at the University of North Carolina, Chapel Hill; faculty research associate at the Department of Strategy & Entrepreneurship, Fuqua School of Business, Duke University; and fellow, Sidney Sussex College, Cambridge University. His main research interests are entrepreneurship, entrepreneurial team formation, gender and entrepreneurship, and evolutionary theory.

Stephanie Delaney, PhD, is the dean of academic programs at South Seattle College. She has been teaching online and hybrid courses and teaching faculty best practices in distance instruction for over 15 years and she is a Quality Matters master reviewer and trainer.

Sarah Egan Warren has been teaching professional communication since 1999. She is an instructor at the Institute for Advanced Analytics at North Carolina State University where she combines her academic and industry experiences to assist graduate students in polishing their communication skills.

Sarah Gaby is a PhD candidate at the University of North Carolina at Chapel Hill. Her research interests include social movements, organizations, and inequality, with a particular focus on youth civic engagement.

Sarah Glova is the founder of Reify Media (reifymedia.com), a media development firm that focuses on digital projects for businesses, education, and training. She's an author, speaker, developer, and self-proclaimed lifelong learner, currently working toward a PhD in Instructional Technology.

Barbi Honeycutt, PhD, is a speaker, scholar, and author. She works with educators to create environments that engage students and improve learning (barbihoneycutt.com). Dr. Honeycutt is the founder of FLIP It Consulting (flipitconsulting.com) and an adjunct faculty member at North Carolina State University.

Claire Howell Major, PhD, is a professor of higher education and department chair of educational leadership, technology, and policy Studies at the University of Alabama. She has authored and co-authored several books, including Learning assessment techniques: A *Handbook for College Faculty* (with Elizabeth Barkley), and *Teaching for Learning: 101 Intentionally Designed Instructional Activities to put Students on the Path to Success* (with Michael Harris and Todd Zakrajsek).

Ron Martinez, PhD, is a professor and researcher in applied linguistics at the Federal University of Paraná in Curitiba, Brazil, where he is also the founder and director of the university writing center, the Academic Publishing Advisory Center ("Centro de Assessoria de Publicação Acadêmica" —CAPA).

Nicki Monahan, MEd, works in faculty development at George Brown College, Toronto, Canada, where she provides training, support, and consultation to help advance the goal "excellence in teaching and learning." As an educational consultant, she has presented widely in both Canada and the U.S. http://nickimonahan.weebly.com/

Penne Restad, PhD, is a distinguished senior lecturer and provost's teaching fellow at the University of Texas at Austin.

Susan Spangler, PhD, taught high school English for 16 years in Illinois before earning a PhD in English Studies. She is an associate professor of English at the State University of New York at Fredonia.

Robert Talbert, PhD, is a professor in the Department of Mathematics at Grand Valley State University in Allendale, Michigan, and a writer, speaker, and consultant on flipped learning in the university. http://rtalbert.org/

Thomas J. Tobin, PhD, is the coordinator of learning technologies in the Center for Teaching and Learning (CTL) at Northeastern Illinois University in Chicago. His latest work is *Evaluating Online Teaching: Implementing Best Practices* (Wiley, 2015) with B. Jean Mandernach and Ann H. Taylor. https://about.me/thomas.j.tobin

Maryellen Weimer, PhD, is a professor emerita of teaching and learning at Penn State Berks. Her books include *Learner-Centered Teaching: Five Key Changes to Practice and Inspired College Teaching: A Career-Long Resource for Professional Growth*. She is the editor of *The Teaching Professor* newsletter and writes a weekly *Teaching Professor* blog.

TOOLS, TEMPLATES, AND CHAPTER RESOURCES

Example of a Guided Practice Assignment for an Online Calculus Course

By Robert Talbert, PhD

Context: This is a guided practice given to an online calculus course that introduces a week-long unit on instantaneous rate of change. Students worked on this assignment in their individual spaces for two days before coming together in an online discussion board to discuss their answers to the exercises and work on more advanced problems.

GUIDED PRACTICE FOR MODULE 2: HOW DO WE CALCULATE CHANGE?

Time estimate to complete this assignment: 2-3 hours

Overview

With this module, our study of calculus begins in earnest. Our main question is: How can we tell how fast a moving object is going at a single point in time, if all we have is information about its location at a given time? By the end of this module, you'll have the tools to answer this question and apply it to problems that don't involve actual moving objects — you'll be able to use the amount of a quantity to find out how fast it's changing.

We'll do this in two steps. First, we will build off of last module's notion of average velocity to introduce the concept of instantaneous velocity and a numerical process for finding instantaneous velocity. Then, we will study that process itself and formalize it in the concept of the limit. This process is central for computing instantaneous velocities, and it will lead us to the main concepts of calculus. For now, we will define the concept of the limit and calculate limits using graphical and numerical methods.

Learning Objectives and Learning Targets

Basic objectives

- Explain the difference between average velocity and instantaneous velocity and the meaning of a negative velocity.
- Explain the meaning of the notation: in clear terms.
- Calculate limits of functions (or determine if a function fails to have

a limit) by examining a graph of the function.

- Calculate limits of functions (or determine if a function fails to have a limit) by constructing a table of values for the function (see Example 1.2).

Advanced objectives

- Use the second average velocity formula to find the average velocity of an object on an interval starting at time and ending at time , where is given but is a variable. Express the answer in simplest form as a function of .
- Given the average velocity of an object from time to time , find its instantaneous velocity at the single moment . (See Example 1.1 and Screencast 1.1.3.)
- Evaluate a limit of an expression that involves fractions algebraically, by simplifying the fraction and "taking limits". (See Activity 1.4.)
- Apply the concept of a limit to find the instantaneous velocity of a moving object, by evaluating a limit of an average velocity.

Learning targets introduced in this module

- 1B (CORE): I can find the limit of a function at a point using numerical, graphical, and symbolic methods.
- 1C: I can find the instantaneous rate of change in a function using limits.

Learning Resources

- Reading: Read the remainder of Active Calculus Section 1.1, from pages 3--7; then read Active Calculus Section 1.2, pages 11--19.
- Video: Watch the following videos from the MTH 201 playlist:
  - Screencast 1.1.3: Finding instantaneous velocity (14:02)
  - Screencast 1.2.1: Limits (6:01)
  - Screencast 1.2.2: Limits of functions using graphing tools (6:27)
  - Screencast 1.2.3: Limits of functions using tables (5:58)
  - Screencast 1.2.4: Limits of functions using spreadsheets (5:38)

Exercises

Reminder: These are to be done in your notes first, then put your responses in the Google Form linked in the "Submission Instructions" area below.

1. In your own words, what is the difference between average velocity and instantaneous velocity?

2. There is a multiple choice item on the submission form that asks you to choose an interpretation of a velocity with negative value. Please answer that question there on the form.
3. On Desmos, there is a graph with some points plotted on it along with two questions to answer: https://www.desmos.com/calculator/jkh3pkp6gn. Do the tasks indicated on Desmos; it will ask you to enter two things into the submission form below.
4. Again on Desmos, there is set of three graphs along with three questions for you to answer: https://www.desmos.com/calculator/yswhby2kdz Do the (three) tasks indicated at Desmos and then put your responses on the response form.

Submission Instructions

Please do your work in your notes, and then submit the results using this form: http://bit.ly/1SOwxRD

Example of an Assessment and Grading Rubric for Group Work

By Claire Howell Major

Grading small group work can be a challenge. Most instructors use a combination of individual product and group product, often developing a percentage split based upon the assignment (e.g. 70 percent individual work and 30 percent group work).

Many instructors also assess the processes of group work. They often do so by asking students to complete group and self-assessment. Following are sample forms for process assessment.

Sample Peer Evaluation Form for Small Group Work

The team member	Needs Improvement = 1	Adequate = 2	Outstanding = 3
Prepares			
Listens			
Contributes			
Respects others			
Demonstrates the following skills:			
Critical thinking			
Problem solving			
Communication			
Decision making			
Subtotals			
Total			

Sample Self-Evaluation Form for Small Group Work

Name _____

Group Number or ID _____

Project Title _____

Rate yourself on your performance on the project using the following scale:
5 = Always; 4 = Frequently; 3 = Sometimes; 2 = Rarely; 1 = Never

Performance Criteria	Rating
I was prepared to contribute to the group	
I stayed on task	
I listened to others	
I participated in discussion	
I encouraged others to participate	
Overall I felt my performance in the group should be rated:	

FLIP a Learning Environment Lesson Plan Template

Date for Lesson: _____

Topic of Lesson/Event: _____

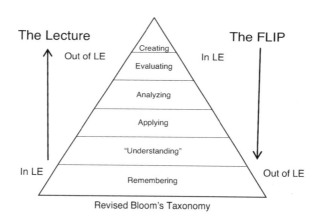

The Lecture   The FLIP

Out of LE   In LE

Creating

Evaluating

Analyzing

Applying

"Understanding"

In LE   Out of LE

Remembering

Revised Bloom's Taxonomy

Action verbs to get started:
Creating: combining, rearranging, producing, planning
Evaluating: critiquing, judging, reviewing, testing, defending
Analyzing: comparing, organizing, connecting, examining
Applying: implementing, using, playing, demonstrating
"Understanding": describing, explaining, summarizing, discussing
Remembering: defining, listing, memorizing, recalling, repeating

Purpose: What do the learners need to be able to do at the end of this lesson?

Learners will be able to [begin with action verb]. _____

_____

_____

PRIOR TO COMING TO LE Learning Outcomes: [Choose activities that address a lower level of Bloom's Taxonomy than you will use in the LE.]

Learners will be able to _____

_____

_____

OUT OF LE

To achieve the outcome(s), learners are [What are learners doing to prepare?]

_____

_____

INTRODUCTION When learners arrive to LE, what are they doing? How will the lesson begin? [What is the Focusing Activity?] _____

_____

_____

_____

Now go back and refer to the purpose of the lesson. Write your learning outcomes and plan the activities.

Learning Outcome: [Choose activities that address a higher level of Bloom's Taxonomy than you used for the "out of LE" LOs.] Learners will be able to

_____

_____

IN THE LE

To achieve this outcome, learners are: [What are learners doing during the session in the LE to achieve this outcome?] _____

_____

_____

_____

Learning Outcome: [Choose activities that address a higher level of Bloom's Taxonomy than you used for the "out of LE" LOs.] Learners will be able to

_____

_____

IN THE LE _____

To achieve this outcome, learners are: [What are the learners doing during the session in the LE to achieve this outcome?] _____

_____

_____

_____

Learning Outcome: [Chose activities that address a higher level of Bloom's Taxonomy than you used for the "out of LE" LOs.] Learners will be able to

_____

_____

IN THE LE _____

To achieve this outcome, learners are: [What are the learners doing during the session in the LE to achieve this outcome?]_____

_____

_____

_____

CLOSING How will the lesson end? [What does the learner need to do to show you they "get it"? What is the next step?]

_____

_____

_____

Remember, the end of this lesson plan can be the beginning of the next.

Assessment Mapping Grid

Use this worksheet to map your learning outcomes, teaching strategies, and assessment activities. Write your learning outcomes from the lesson plan in column 2. Then fill in the rest of the grid.

Topic: _____

Purpose/Goal: _____

30,000 ft view ◄———► 3 ft view

COLUMN 1	COLUMN 2	COLUMN 3	COLUMN 4
Summative Assessment (Begin with the end.)	**Learning Outcomes**	**Teaching and Learning Strategies**	**Formative Assessment**
Students will demonstrate mastery by:	At the end of this lesson, students will be able to:	Students will do this by:	Students will practice and receive feedback by:
	LO #1:		
	LO #2:		
	LO #3:		

Step 2: Assessment Worksheet

Use this worksheet to focus on planning your assessment activities before, during, and after class time. (1) Write your learning outcomes in the middle column. (2) Make a plan for each learning outcome and teaching strategy. Do activities belong in class or out of class? How could you assess each one? Do you need to assess each one?

Topic: _____

Purpose/Goal of Lesson: _____

Out of Class (Formative Assessment)		Learning Outcomes	In Class (Formative Assessment)	
How could this LO be assessed outside of class?	What could students do before or after class?	What do students need to do to achieve the goal?	What could students do during class?	How could this LO be assessed during class?
		LO #1:		
		LO #2:		
		LO #3:		

TIP! These two columns will become the lesson plan flipped class.

Additional Resources

If you enjoyed this book, Magna Publications has additional resources for you:

BULK PURCHASES

To purchase multiple print copies of this book, please visit:
www.MagnaGroupBooks.com

BOOKS

Grading Strategies for the Online College Classroom:
A Collection of Faculty Articles
Written and designed by educators with online faculty in mind, *Grading Strategies for the Online College Classroom* will challenge readers to reflect on their current grading strategies, inspire them to consider changes to promote student engagement and success, and prepare them with the tools and ideas to begin today.

Teaching Strategies for the Online College Classroom:
A Collection of Faculty Articles
This book covers many topics relevant to both new-to-online and experienced online teachers, plus it includes references and recommended resources. It is a great starting place for anyone involved in the online learning community and anyone interested in improving their online offerings.

Essential Teaching Principles:
A Resource Collection for Adjunct Faculty
https://www.amazon.com/dp/B01HSEC0V2
This book provides a wealth of both research-driven and classroom-tested best practices to help adjuncts develop the knowledge and skills required to run a successful classroom.

Teaching Strategies for the College Classroom:
A Collection of Faculty Articles
http://amzn.to/Yas3NE
Practical classroom-tested "tool kit" for faculty members who would like to develop their teaching practice. Contains concrete pedagogical strategies that have been tested in the authors' classrooms and together form a handbook of classroom strategies—an important resource for faculty at all career stages.

Grading Strategies for the College Classroom:
A Collection of Articles for Faculty
http://amzn.to/15RhFLX
This book provides insights into managing the complicated task of assigning a simple letter to a semester's work. It's a must-read for any faculty member seeking to understand how to use assessment to measure and enhance performance.

SUBSCRIPTIONS

Faculty Focus
www.facultyfocus.com
A free e-newsletter on effective teaching strategies for the college classroom, featuring a weekly blog post from Maryellen Weimer, PhD.

The Teaching Professor Newsletter
www.TeachingProfessorNewsletter.com
Published ten times a year, The Teaching Professor features ideas, insights, and best pedagogical practices written for and by educators who are passionate about teaching. Edited by Maryellen Weimer, PhD.

Online Classroom Newsletter
www.OnlineClassroomNewsletter.com
Published twelve times a year, Online Classroom helps you understand the current trends, challenges, ideas, and pedagogical insights for effective online instruction. Edited by John Orlando, PhD.

20-Minute Mentor Commons
http://bit.ly/2biCIR3
20-Minute Mentor Commons gives your entire campus unlimited, on-demand access to a library of Magna 20-Minute Mentor programs. This resource continues to grow as more programs are added regularly. They feature the top experts in higher education ready to answer pressing questions whenever, and wherever, your faculty need answers.

CONFERENCES

The Teaching Professor Conference

www.TeachingProfessor.com
This annual event provides an opportunity to learn effective pedagogical techniques, hear from leading teaching experts, and interact with colleagues committed to teaching and learning excellence.

The Teaching Professor Technology Conference

www.TeachingProfessorTechnologyConference.com
This conference examines the technologies that are changing the way teachers teach and students learn, while giving special emphasis to the pedagogically effective ways you can harness these new technologies in your courses and on your campus.

Leadership in Higher Education Conference

www.magnapubs.com/2016-leadership-in-higher-education-conference/
As members of the academic community are tasked with greater accountability than ever before, effective leadership is a highly desired, competitive trait. The Leadership in Higher Education Conference puts the tools in your hands to develop professionally, exposes you to ideas and strategies that you can apply at your own school, and boosts your career progress.

Made in the USA
Columbia, SC
02 June 2018